COMPAN TRAVEL GUIDE TO

CUSCO, PERU

Must See, Must Do Activities! Top Attractions! insider and Local Tips! Cultural Immersion!

CARL DIAZ

COPYRIGHT NOTICE

SCAN HERE TO GAIN
ACCESS TO ALL MY BOOKS

DISCLAIMER

Please note that the information contained within this document is for educational purposes only. The information contained herein has been obtained from sources believed to be reliable at the time of publication. The opinions expressed herein are subject to change without notice. Readers acknowledge that the Author / Publisher is not engaging in rendering legal, financial or professional advice.

The Publisher / Author disclaims all warranties as to the accuracy, completeness, or adequacy of such information.

The Publisher assumes no liability for errors, omissions, or inadequacies in the information contained herein or from the interpretations thereof. The publisher / Author specifically disclaims any liability from the use or application of the information contained herein or from the interpretations thereof.

Table of Contents

INTRODUCTION

Hola, amigos! Welcome to the heart of the Andes, my tiny world, where I'll tell you all about the lovely city of Cusco, Peru. I'm pleased to be your guide on this magnificent adventure through ancient history, breathtaking scenery, and the welcoming embrace of Peruvian culture. After spending a lot of time navigating the cobblestone streets and discovering Cusco's hidden jewels, I'm delighted to tell you all about this magical place.

About Cusco

Welcome to Cusco, where the whispers of ancient civilizations reverberate through the Andean air and the mystical aura of the Inca Empire remains. Cusco, located at an amazing altitude of 3,400 meters (11,000 feet) above sea level, is a living witness to the harmonious blend of Inca and Spanish influences that molded its rich past.

The Inca's Legacy

Cusco was once the beating center of the powerful Inca Empire, serving as the cultural and political hub that linked South America's vast lands. Wandering through the Historic District, you'll be surrounded by intricately carved stone walls, remains of an advanced civilization that thrived in the Andes.

Plaza de Armas: A Timeless Gathering Place

The Plaza de Armas is central to Cusco's tale, a magnificent area that has witnessed centuries of history. The Cathedral of Santo Domingo, a remarkable specimen of colonial architecture, stands boldly here, its ornate façade symbolising the collision and merging of two worlds. Take a leisurely stroll around the square, where locals and visitors mingle, creating a lively tapestry of life.

The Quechua Connection

Immerse yourself in the local culture by learning Quechua, an indigenous language that is still used in Cusco's streets. While Spanish is commonly spoken, learning a few Quechua phrases gives a personal touch to your travels and creates connections with the friendly inhabitants. The sounds of merchants chatting in Quechua fill the air throughout the marketplaces, serving as a reminder of the region's continuing legacy.

Traditional Markets: A Kaleidoscope of Culture

Venture into the bustling markets, such as San Pedro Market, where an explosion of colors and scents awaits. Artisans proudly display handwoven textiles, delicate pottery, and vivid alpaca wool goods. Engage with the vendors, learn about the significance of each piece, and possibly negotiate a reasonable price - this is more than simply a transaction; it's a cultural exchange.

Altitude and Acclimatization

When you arrive in Cusco, you'll instantly become acquainted with its high-altitude location. The air may be thinner and the sun more fierce, but don't worry; acclimation is part of the trip. Take it easy on the first day, sipping coca tea, a native treatment for altitude sickness, and allowing your body to adjust gradually.

San Blas: The Bohemian Quarter.

Wander through the narrow streets of San Blas to experience Cusco's creative essence. Known as the "artist's quarter," this bohemian enclave emanates creativity at every opportunity. Admire the works of local painters and sculptors, and consider participating in a workshop to make your own piece of Andean art.

Festivals and Celebrations

Cusco's calendar is filled with bright festivals that bring the city to life via music, dance, and colorful processions. One of the most important events is Inti Raymi, or the Festival of the Sun, which takes place in June. Witnessing this ancient Inca ceremony at the historic Sacsayhuaman is like traveling back in time, as the sun deity is worshiped in a pageant of tradition and reverence.

Inti Raymi, A Sun-Kissed Spectacle

The Inti Raymi festival unfolds in a grand theatrical production, with actors donning elaborate costumes to reenact sacred rituals. The excitement is apparent as locals and visitors alike gather to appreciate the sun's warmth and life-giving energy. It is an experience that spans time, linking the present to Cusco's ancient roots.

Weather and Seasons

Understanding Cusco's seasons is essential for arranging an optimal visit. The dry season, which runs from May to October, provides bright skies and comfortable temperatures, making it the best time to travel. However, if you prefer a more tranquil experience and lush scenery, the rainy season, which lasts from

November to April, covers the region in brilliant greens.

The Dance of Seasons

Witness the transformation of the scenery during the rainy season, when terraced fields and valleys bloom with verdant magnificence. Though rain showers are frequent, they are usually brief, giving way to beautiful rainbows that arch across the sky - a monument to Cusco's ever-changing but captivating weather.

Getting to Know the Culture

Now, let us dig into the rich tapestry of Cusco culture. To completely immerse yourself in the local experience, you must learn the intricacies and embrace the traditions.

Connect with locals.

Cusco's heart rests not just in its breathtaking architecture and historical sites, but also in the kindness of its people. Engage in talks with locals, and you'll notice a real desire to share their story. While Spanish is the primary language, trying a few phrases in Quechua might be a fun icebreaker. Locals appreciate the effort, and it adds a human dimension to your relationships.

Embrace the markets.

Cusco's markets are vibrant hubs of activity, showcasing the artistry and craftsmanship of the region. Spend some time roaming around the San Pedro Market, where the colorful kiosks provide a sensory assault of sights, sounds, and fragrances. Local craftsmen proudly display their handwoven textiles, beautiful pottery, and traditional clothes. Take advantage of the opportunity to haggle - it is more than just a transaction; it is a cultural dance that adds authenticity to your purchases.

Participate at festivals.

Cusco enjoys celebrating, and the city celebrates several festivals throughout the year.

If your visit coincides with a local festival, consider yourself fortunate. The streets are bustling with parades, music, and traditional dances. The most famous event is Inti Raymi, or the event of the Sun, which takes place in late June. It's a spectacular show reenacting an ancient Inca ceremonial, complete with colorful costumes and processions.

Learn about Andean Cosmovision.

To properly understand Cusco's culture, become acquainted with Andean cosmovision. This worldview, which is profoundly founded in Inca traditions, sees the universe as a harmonious interplay of physical and spiritual realms. This belief system influences many elements of daily living, including rites and ceremonies. Local guides frequently share insights into the cosmovision on tours, improving your understanding of the cultural fabric that runs across Cusco.

Traditional Clothing and Textiles

As you go across the city, you'll find many inhabitants proudly wearing traditional clothes. Each costume, embellished with brilliant colors and intricate designs, represents the wearer's cultural identity and, in many cases, their hometown. Take a time to recognize the craftsmanship and significance of these clothing. If you're searching for a meaningful souvenir, consider buying handmade textiles directly from local craftsmen to support their work and help preserve this piece of Cusco's cultural legacy.

Culinary traditions

Food is an essential component of any culture, and Cusco's gastronomic scene reflects its unique history. Dive into the local cuisine by trying traditional meals like rocoto relleno (stuffed spicy pepper), cuy al horno (roasted guinea pig), and quinoa soup. Don't pass up the opportunity to attend a traditional Pachamanca, a ceremonial feast in which food is cooked underground using hot stones - a gourmet experience that goes beyond taste and immerses you in ancient customs.

Art and Music

Cusco's streets are filled with traditional Andean music, played on instruments such as the panpipe and charango. Local art galleries exhibit contemporary and indigenous art, offering a look into the city's creative spirit. Attending a live music performance or viewing an art exhibition will help you connect with Cusco's artistic manifestations.

By actively engaging with the culture, participating in local traditions, and appreciating the daily rhythms of life, you will discover that Cusco's cultural allure extends far beyond its historical sites; it is a living, breathing experience that will stay with you long after you leave these ancient streets.

Cusco takes you on a journey through time, where ancient and modern meet in a perfect dance. As we embark on this comprehensive guide to Cusco, let the spirit of the Andes guide your steps. From the cobblestone streets of the Historic District to the breathtaking views of Sacsayhuaman, every nook of Cusco has a tale to tell. So buckle your seatbelts, dear adventurers; the wonders of Cusco await!

Chapter 1

ESSENTIAL PREPARATIONS

Travel Planning

Before we dig into the vivid tapestry of Cusco, let's make sure you're prepared for a wonderful adventure. Timing is crucial, and in Cusco, the seasons can influence your experience. Consider walking around ancient ruins in the bright sun or sipping cocoa tea while the rain falls on your window. It all depends on when you want to travel.

Best time to visit

Welcome to Cusco, where the weather is as unique as its culture. Choosing the ideal time to visit this historical site might greatly improve your overall experience. Here's a summary of the Cusco seasons:

DRY SEASON (MAY TO SEPTEMBER):

Advantages:

- **Clear skies**: During these months, the sky are mostly clear, allowing for uninterrupted views of the breathtaking landscapes and ancient monuments.

- **Ideal for Trekking:** If the Inca Trail or other trekking activities are on your itinerary, now is the time to lace up your hiking boots. The pathways are dry, so you can enjoy the journey without becoming muddy.

Popular Activities:

- **Machu Picchu Exploration:** The dry season is ideal for visiting Machu Picchu, ensuring that your classic images are not marred by rain clouds.

- **Outdoor Festivals:** Many traditional festivals, such as the Virgen de la Asuncion in August, are held during this time, providing a one-of-a-kind cultural experience.

Considerations:

- **High Tourist Season:** As expected, this is the peak tourist season. While the weather is wonderful, popular attractions might become packed. To get the greatest deals, book your accommodations and trips ahead of time.

RAINY SEASON (NOVEMBER TO MARCH):

Advantages:

- **Lush Landscapes:** During the rainy season, Cusco becomes a lush, green paradise. The sceneries come to life, and the surroundings are a stunning spectacle.

- **Fewer crowds:** There are fewer tourists than during the dry season. As a result, you may have more privacy at some of the popular sites.

Popular Activities:

- **Photography opportunities:** The bright colors of the landscapes during this season provide unique and beautiful photographic opportunity.

- **Indoor Explorations:** While outside activities may be limited, this is a wonderful opportunity to visit the city's museums and indoor attractions.

Considerations:

- **Rainfall and Mud:** Expect periodic rain showers, and certain trekking trails may be muddy. Waterproof gear and sturdy boots are recommended.

- **Limited Accessibility:** Due to weather conditions, some paths or routes leading to specific places may be temporarily closed.

IN-BETWEEN SEASONS (APRIL AND OCTOBER):

Advantages:

- **Balanced weather**: April and October are transitional months, with a mix of dry and rainy days. You can get a taste of both worlds.

Popular Activities:

- **Varied Experiences:** Explore outdoor attractions on clear days and embrace the refreshing rain on others. It's an ideal time for diverse adventures.

Considerations:

- **Variable Conditions:** Pack for shifting weather. Layers are your best friend during these transitional times.

GENERAL WEATHER TIPS:

- **Altitude Adjustment:** Remember that Cusco is at a high altitude. Take it easy for the first several days to adjust to the altitude and avoid altitude sickness.

- **Sun Protection:** Regardless of the season, the sun can be harsh at high elevations. Bring sunscreen, a hat, and sunglasses to protect your skin from the sun's rays.

- **Hydration:** Altitude can lead to dehydration. Drink plenty of water, especially if you are participating in vigorous activities such as trekking.

In conclusion, the best time to visit Cusco is largely dependent on your tastes. If you want clear skies and good trekking conditions, the dry season is great. However, if you enjoy bright scenery and don't mind the odd rain, the rainy season has its own appeal. The transitional months provide a good balance of both. Armed with this knowledge, you can confidently plan your trip to Cusco, assuring a personalized experience.

Visa and Entry Requirements

Let's get down to business and make sure your arrival in Cusco goes as smoothly as a cup of mate de coca.

Visa requirements

Cusco, as part of Peru, welcomes tourists from a variety of countries without requiring a visa for visits of up to 90 days. However, it's essential to double-check the specific entry requirements for your nationality before packing those bags. A visit to the official website of the Peruvian Consulate or Embassy in your own country should provide the most current and correct information.

Tourist Card

When you arrive at Jorge Chávez International Airport in Lima or Alejandro Velasco Astete International Airport in Cusco, you'll be given a little, blue Andean immigration card. This card, also known as a tourist card, should be filled out with your personal information and kept safe throughout your stay. Immigration officers will stamp it upon entering, and you must provide it before exiting the country.

Extension of Stay

If you're having so much fun that you want to prolong your stay beyond the initial 90-day period, that's an option. However, it is recommended that you ask for an extension before the original 90 days elapse. Extensions are often given for up to an additional 90 days, but the procedure can take some time, so prepare beforehand.

Visa for Work or Study

Those planning a longer stay in Cusco, possibly for business or study, will need a different sort of visa. The specifics vary depending on your goals, and it is strongly advisable to contact the Peruvian Consulate well in advance. They can help you navigate the application procedure, which frequently includes sending supporting documents like a job offer or evidence of enrollment from an educational school.

Yellow Fever Vaccination

While a yellow fever vaccination is not required for entry, travelers should check to see if they need one before traveling in Cusco. If you have recently visited a country where yellow fever is present, you may be asked to produce proof of vaccination upon entry.

Travel Insurance

Though it is not a direct entry requirement, obtaining comprehensive travel insurance is a wise decision. This insurance can be a lifesaver in unexpected circumstances, covering medical crises, trip cancellations, and lost luggage. Ensure that your policy covers high-altitude places and adventurous activities such as trekking.

Currency and Customs Declaration

Before arriving in Cusco, educate yourself with the Peruvian Sol (PEN). It is good to keep some local cash on hand for modest transactions or transportation. Also, be prepared to report any considerable quantities of currency or valuables upon entering, as customs officers may inquire about them.

Remember that visa and entry procedures are subject to change, so stay up to speed on the latest information from official government sources to guarantee a smooth entry into the lovely land of Cusco.

Packing Tips:

Okay, let's talk about packing - the art of blending comfort, style, and preparedness. Cusco's altitude (3,399 meters or 11,152 feet) is no joke, and you'll need to be prepared for everything from sun-soaked ruins to freezing mountain evenings.

- **Layers, layers, layers!**

Cusco's weather is like a mood ring; it changes regularly. The days can be warm, but the nights can be extremely cold. Pack flexible layers that may be quickly added or removed. A light jacket or sweater is your best friend, especially when the sun wants to play hide-and-seek.

- **Comfortable walking shoes.**

Cobbled streets and uneven terrain are common in Cusco. Whether you're visiting ancient ruins or wandering through the Plaza de Armas, good, durable walking shoes are essential. Save the cute but impractical footwear for a future journey.

- **Altitude Sickness Remedies**

Cusco is at a dizzying altitude, and altitude sickness is a serious worry. Pack over-the-counter medications like acetazolamide (Diamox) or natural alternatives like coca tea to help your body adjust. Stay hydrated and listen to your body; slow and steady wins the race.

- **Sun Protection Essentials.**

At high altitudes, the sun can be quite bright. Pack a wide-brimmed hat, UV-protective sunglasses, and high-SPF sunscreen. Trust me when I suggest that visiting open-air sites like Sacsayhuaman or Machu Picchu will be worthwhile.

- **Daypack for Excursions.**

A tiny, comfortable daypack can make all the difference on day outings and treks. It should be large enough to accommodate water, snacks, a camera, and your layers. Bonus points if it includes compartments to keep things tidy.

- **Rain gear for unpredictable weather.**

Cusco's weather can be unpredictable, particularly from November to March. A small, waterproof jacket or poncho protects you from unexpected rain showers. It's preferable to be safe than soggy, right?

- **Adapter and Powerbank**

A universal adapter for Peru's electrical outlets can keep your gadgets running smoothly. Cusco is highly photogenic, so don't miss out on photographing those magnificent moments. A dependable power bank keeps your devices charged for the ideal shot.

- **Small First Aid Kit**

While pharmacies are easily available, a little first-aid kit can come in handy. Include essential supplies such as bandages, pain relievers, and any personal medications. Altitude-related headaches are common, so be ready.

- **Reusable Water Bottle and Snacks**

Stay hydrated, my friend. The altitude can sneak up on you, so bring a reusable water bottle. Include some energy-boosting snacks, such as almonds or granola bars, for a quick boost while exploring.

- **Comfortable Day-to-Night Attire**

Cusco's cold evenings require a stylish yet comfortable layer, so dress accordingly. Consider packing an outfit that can effortlessly shift from day to night. A good blouse or shirt teamed with comfortable pants can do the trick.

- **Document Organizer**

Keep your critical paperwork (passport, tickets, and reservations) organized and easily accessible. A travel wallet or organizer provides extra convenience, especially while you're on the go.

Remember, the goal is to create a balance between readiness and adaptability. Pack smartly, expect the unexpected, and prepare to go on a journey through Cusco's beautiful landscapes and rich history.

Chapter 2

NAVIGATING CUSCO

Now that you've decided to visit Cusco, let's talk about how to move around this fascinating city. From navigating the crowded streets to discovering hidden gems, I have you covered. So, fasten your seatbelts (metaphorically, of course), and let's have a look at how to get around Cusco.

Getting There

Air option

Choosing Your Arrival Point:

Cusco is well-connected, and selecting the best arrival point can improve your travel experience. Consider the choices below:

Alejandro Velasco Astete International Airport (Cuz):

- **Convenience:** Located around 10 minutes from the city center, this airport serves as the primary entrance for the majority of travelers.
- **Domestic Flights:** If you're already in Peru, connecting flights from major cities such as Lima make this an easy option.

Alternative airports:

- **Juliaca Airport(JUL):** Juliaca, located further away, is an option for visitors touring Peru's southern regions before traveling to Cusco.

Air Travel Tips:

Altitude considerations:

- **Gradual Ascent:** If possible, plan a gradual ascent to acclimate your body to Cusco's high altitude.

- **Stay Hydrated:** Drink plenty of water to alleviate any altitude-related problems.

Book Flights:

- **Flexibility:** Consider flexible travel dates to take advantage of lower fares. Mid-week flights frequently provide better value.
- **Connecting Flights**: Look at possibilities with layovers in Lima or other Peruvian cities to potentially save money.

Transportation from the airport:

- **Pre-book Transfers:** To make your arrival easier, consider scheduling airport transfers that will take you directly to your accommodation.
- **Taxis and rideshares:** Official taxis and rideshare services are available for a more convenient trip into the city.

Land and Rail Options:

Train to Cusco:

- **Scenic Routes:** Some travelers opt for scenic train journeys from cities like Ollantaytambo to Cusco. Although longer, these routes provide spectacular scenery.

Bus services:

Long-distance buses connect Cusco with other cities. While inexpensive, be prepared for longer journey durations.

Pre-Arrival Checklist:

Documentation:

- **Passport:** Make sure your passport is valid for at least six months after your scheduled departure date.
- **Visa Requirements:** Check and fulfill any visa requirements for entering Peru.

Vaccination and Health Precautions:

- **Routine Vaccinations:** Ensure routine vaccinations are up-to-date.
- **Altitude Medication:** Speak with a healthcare practitioner about altitude sickness prevention.

Currency and Payment methods:

- **Local Currency**: It is advised to have some Peruvian soles on hand for early expenses.
- **Credit Cards:** To avoid card difficulties, inform your bank of your travel dates.

Weather-appropriate Clothing:

- **Layered Clothing:** Cusco's weather can vary. Pack layers to accommodate temperature variations.
- **Comfortable Footwear:** Bring comfortable walking shoes to explore the city.

Local Etiquette and Customs:

- **Language Basics:** Learn a few fundamental Spanish phrases to help you communicate.
- **Respect Local Customs:** Familiarize oneself with local norms to demonstrate respect during your stay.

The journey to Cusco is the thrilling beginning of your Peruvian vacation. Whether you arrive by flight, train, or bus, careful planning and a sense of exploration will ensure a great stay in this interesting city.

Transportation Tango

Airport Transfers

As I landed in Alejandro Velasco Astete International Airport, the gateway to Cusco, the excitement bubbled up.

Understanding The Airport

The major gateway to Cusco is Alejandro Velasco Astete International Airport. This airport, located about 3.7 miles (6 kilometers) from the city center, has a stunning view of the Andes Mountains. While it is a small airport, it acts as an important hub for tourists visiting Cusco and the surrounding areas.

Transportation Options from the Airport

- **Taxis:** For a seamless transition from the airport to your accommodation, consider using authorized airport taxis. These are safe and easily accessible. Before you get in the taxi, make sure it has a visible identification badge and a clear pricing structure.

- **Private Transfers:** Many hotels offer private transfer services, providing a convenient and personalized option. This is especially useful if you have a late arrival or early departure, ensuring a stress-free ride.

- **Airport Shuttles:** Shared shuttle services are available and affordable, especially if you're traveling in a group. They make many stops, making it a somewhat longer but more sociable method to get to your destination.

Tips for Airport Transfers

- **Altitude Awareness:** Cusco is situated at a high altitude (3,399 meters or 11,152 feet). If you are sensitive to altitude, notify your driver. Take it easy, stay hydrated, and let your body adjust.

- **Pre-Book Transfers:** To make your arrival easier, consider pre-booking your transfer online. This saves time and assures a seamless start to your Cusco experience.

- **Currency Exchange:** Keep a little quantity of local currency on hand for the transfer. While most establishments accept credit cards, having some Peruvian soles on hand can be useful for gratuities or small purchases.

Public Transport

Navigating Cusco's Public Transportation System

Cusco's public transportation system consists of buses and colectivos (shared taxis). While not as vast as other big cities, it is a cost-effective method to tour the city and its surroundings.

Buses

- **Local Buses:** Cusco has a network of local buses serving various neighborhoods. Buses are inexpensive, but routes can be difficult to navigate. Don't be afraid to ask locals or seek assistance from your lodging.

- **Tourist Buses:** Some firms provide tourist-oriented bus services that take you to popular locations while delivering interesting commentary. These provide an excellent overview of the city and its surrounds.

- **Colectivos (shared taxis):** Colectivos, identifiable by their distinctive colors, travel on designated routes, picking up passengers along the way. They are inexpensive and can be flagged down on the street or at specific stops.

- **Route Information:** Discover the routes and locations served by colectivos. This can be obtained from locals, online sources, or your lodging. Colectivos are a great way to get a sense of the local rhythm in Cusco.

Tips for Public Transport

- **Peak Hours:** Be mindful of peak commuting hours, especially in the morning and evening. Public transportation can become congested, and traffic may hinder your route.

- **Exact Change:** If using a bus or colectivo, aim to have exact change. Small denominations are welcomed, as drivers may not have change for larger notes.

- **Language Barrier:** Although English is not generally spoken, knowing a few basic Spanish phrases will help you communicate with drivers and other passengers.

Walking Tours

Discover Cusco at Your Own Pace.

Walking tours in Cusco provide an intimate and immersive experience for discovering the city's charming streets, rich history, and vibrant culture. Lace up your walking shoes, take a map, and let the cobblestone paths guide you around this Andean treasure.

Self-guided walking routes

- **Historic District and Plaza de Armas Exploration:**

Highlights:

Begin your adventure at the Plaza de Armas, Cusco's core. Admire the Cathedral of Santo Domingo and Qorikancha (Temple of the Sun), which both feature a mix of Inca and colonial architecture.

Insider Tip: Take your time exploring the neighboring neighborhoods, uncovering hidden gems such as local markets and artisan workshops.

- **San Blas Neighborhood Stroll:**

Highlights:

Venture into the bohemian San Blas neighborhood, known for its narrow streets, art galleries, and the San Blas Church. Enjoy panoramic views of Cusco from the iconic San Blas Plaza.

Insider Tip: Visit the studios of local artists to see traditional craftsmanship and possibly discover a unique keepsake.

- **Sacsayhuaman Pathway:**

Highlights:

Embark on a scenic walk to the ancient Inca fortress of Sacsayhuaman. The walk provides amazing views of Cusco and its neighboring mountains.

Insider Tip: Plan your visit for late afternoon to catch the golden hues of the sunset giving a magnificent glow over the historic monument.

Guided walking tours

- **Cusco City Tours:**

Highlights:

Take a guided tour to learn more about Cusco's history and culture. Knowledgeable guides add context to sights such as the Plaza de Armas, providing a more complete experience.

Insider Tip: Choose trips that include visits to lesser-known locations, which will provide a more comprehensive understanding of Cusco's legacy.

- **Machu Picchu Preparatory Walk**

Highlights:

Prepare for your Machu Picchu experience by taking guided hikes that imitate hiking conditions. These hikes adapt you to the altitude and provide a taste of the spectacular scenery.

Insider Tip: Use these walks not just for physical preparation, but also to meet other tourists and share information and excitement about your planned Machu Picchu visit.

Practical Tips for Walking Tours

- **Comfortable Footwear:** Cusco's streets are a charming but uneven mix of cobblestones and narrow pathways. To safely cross the terrain, choose comfortable and sturdy footwear.

- **Hydration and Sun Protection:** The sun at high altitudes can be harsh. Carry a refillable water bottle and sunscreen to stay hydrated and protect your skin on your adventures.

- **Photography Opportunities:** Cusco is a photographers' delight. Don't forget your camera or smartphone to capture the vivid street scenes, historical architecture, and magnificent scenery.

- **Respect Local Customs:** Some places, particularly near religious sites, may require modest clothing. As you explore different neighborhoods, be cognizant of local customs and traditions.

- **Join Group Tours for Solo Travelers:** If you're traveling alone, think about joining a group walking tour. It not only improves safety but also allows you to meet other tourists and share your experiences.

Taxis and Rideshare

Navigating Cusco's Streets with Ease Taxi:

- **Identifying Official Taxi:**

Look for official taxi stands or request one from your hotel. Authorized taxis have visible identity badges and a set price structure.

Insider Tip: To ensure safety and fair pricing, avoid using unmarked or unlicensed cabs.

- **Negotiating Fares:**

While most taxis use meters, it's common to negotiate fares for longer journeys or day trips. To avoid misunderstandings, agree on a fare before beginning the journey.

Insider Tip: Ask locals or your hotel for an idea of normal cab prices as a starting point for discussions.

- **Taxi Apps:**

Consider using local taxi apps such as Easy Taxi or Uber, which offer a more convenient and transparent way to book rides.

Insider Tip: To ease the procedure, download the app and create an account before coming in Cusco.

- **Night Travel:**

If traveling at night, opt for radio-dispatched taxis from reputable providers. These promote safer journeys at evening.

Insider Tip: When in doubt, ask your hotel to recommend a reliable cab service.

Rideshare (Uber):

- **Availability and reliability:**

Uber operates in Cusco and offers an alternative to traditional taxis. Availability may be more limited than in major cities, so plan accordingly.

Insider Tip: Check the app's real-time availability and consider regular taxis during peak hours.

- **Payment convenience:**

One advantage of ridesharing apps is their cashless payment approach. Link your credit card to the app for easy transactions.

Insider Tip: To avoid payment troubles, make sure your payment method is properly configured in the app.

- **Language barriers:**

While Uber drivers often speak basic English, knowing some key Spanish phrases can help you communicate clearly.

Insider Tip: Write down the name and address of your destination in Spanish for easier interactions.

- **Shared rides:**

Rideshare apps frequently provide shared trip options for a lesser cost. If you're okay sharing a ride, this can be a cost-effective option.

Insider Tip: Shared journeys may take longer due to additional stops for other passengers.

General Tips for Taxi and Rideshare Travel:

- **Know Your Route:**

Familiarize yourself with typical routes and landmarks to ensure you're on the proper path. Use navigation apps to keep track of your route.

- **Travel in Groups:**

If feasible, share cabs or rideshares with other travelers, especially at late. This provides an additional layer of safety.

- **Cash for Taxi:**

While ridesharing apps allow for cashless transactions, regular cabs may not accept credit cards.

- **Driver recommendations:**

If you have a pleasant experience with a taxi or ridesharing driver, request their contact information. Having a reputable driver's number can be useful for future trips.

- **Riding Responsibly in Cusco**

Environmental Considerations: Cusco, like many other towns, suffers from traffic congestion and poor air quality. Consider sharing rides or using sustainable transportation options when available.

- **Cultural Sensitivity:**

Be respectful of local norms and polite when riding. If the driver is willing to engage in polite conversation, you will have the opportunity to discover more about Cusco's culture from a local perspective.

Chapter 3

ACCOMMODATIONS

Now that you're getting ready for your fantastic vacation to Cusco, let's get into the chapter about selecting the ideal home away from home - hotels. Trust me, it's more than just a place to bed; it's about immersing yourself in the local culture and making your stay as unforgettable as the sites you'll see.

Overview of Accommodation Options.

Cusco welcomes you with a choice of hotel alternatives to suit all types of tourists and budgets. The city offers everything from beautiful boutique hotels to cozy hostels and luxury resorts. Let us break it down:

Boutique Hotels:

- **El Mercado Tunqui.**

Address: Calle Siete Cuartones 306, Cusco.

El Mercado Tunqui, located near the Plaza de Armas, is a hidden gem that flawlessly combines heritage and innovation. This beautiful hotel in a refurbished market building offers an authentic Peruvian experience. Each room is a quiet retreat, decorated with local artwork and fabrics, and the rooftop terrace provides panoramic views of the city. The central position provides easy access to Cusco's major attractions and vibrant atmosphere.

- **Palacio de Inka**

Address: Plazoleta Santo Domingo in Cusco

The Palacio del Inka, a Luxury Collection Hotel in Cusco, emanates colonial beauty. The hotel, located near the Qorikancha, features precisely crafted rooms with Inca characteristics. The courtyard's ancient Inca walls transport you back in time. A spa, gourmet restaurant, and dedicated staff round out the regal experience. Its proximity to important locations makes exploration simple.

- **JW Marriott El Convento Cusco.**

Address: Ruinas 432, Cusco.

The JW Marriott El Convento, located in a 16th-century convent, is a luxurious retreat. The hotel effortlessly combines ancient architecture and modern comforts. The spacious rooms, furnished with Andean décor, offer a peaceful refuge. Enjoy the great dining selections, a spa, and the courtyard, which features nighttime entertainment. With a location near the Plaza de Armas, you're just steps away from Cusco's dynamic atmosphere.

Cozy hostels:

- **Wild Rover Hostel**

Address: Cuesta Santa Ana 758, Cusco.

Wild Rover Hostel is ideal for people looking for a dynamic, social atmosphere. This hostel, located in the San Blas area, offers both dormitories and private rooms. The colorful common areas offer events, live music, and a thriving bar scene. The rooftop patio offers excellent views of the city. It's more than simply lodging; it's a community of fellow travelers who share tales and make memories.

- **Loki Hostel**

Address: Calle Tandapata 161, Cusco

Loki Hostel, located in the middle of Cusco, is a popular destination for backpackers looking for both fun and leisure. The hostel has a variety of lodging alternatives, and the lively bar scene assures a friendly atmosphere. Participate in everyday activities planned by the hostel or relax in the comfortable lounge spaces. The central location enables for convenient exploration of Cusco's attractions.

Luxurious Resorts:

- **Belmond Hotel Monasterio**

Address: Calle Palacios 136, Cusco.

Belmond Hotel Monasterio, located just steps from the Plaza de Armas, is a luxurious masterpiece housed in a former monastery. The hotel's historical beauty is enhanced by exquisite rooms, superb cuisine, and a tranquil garden. Immerse yourself in the unique ambiance and take advantage of the spa's personalized services. This is more than just lodging; it's a trip through time.

- **Tambo del Inka, a Luxury Collection Resort & Spa**

Address: Av. Ferrocarril s/n, Sacred Valley

Tambo del Inka, located in the Sacred Valley, is the height of luxury. This resort overlooks the

Vilcanota River and provides an enchanting escape. Enjoy spacious rooms, exquisite cuisine, and spa treatments. The outdoor pool and balcony offer a panoramic view of the surrounding mountains. It's a getaway inside a retreat, thanks to its calm setting.

Choosing the Right Neighborhood.

Cusco's neighborhoods each have their own characteristics, so choosing the correct one improves your whole experience. Let me walk you through some of the key areas:

Historic District

Nestled at the heart of Cusco, the Historic District is like stepping into a living museum. This region is defined by its cobblestone streets, centuries-old cathedrals, and bustling marketplaces. Staying here puts you within walking distance of the historic Plaza de Armas, where history comes alive.

Advantages:

- **Proximity to Top Attractions:** The Cathedral of Santo Domingo, Qorikancha (Temple of the Sun), and the bustling San Pedro Market are all nearby.

Recommended accommodations:

- **"El Mercado Tunqui":** Located at Calle Siete Cuartones 306, this boutique hotel complements the district's historic beauty. It makes an excellent base for exploration.

Tip: This neighborhood can get fairly lively, especially during festivals, and provides an immersive view of Cusco's traditional celebrations.

San Blas

Ascending the hills from the Historic District, you'll find San Blas – the artsy quarter of Cusco.

It's known for its bohemian ambiance, tiny lanes, and plethora of artisan workshops, making it a paradise for those looking for a more relaxed vibe.

Advantages:

- **Art and Culture:** Discover local artists' studios, quaint galleries, and cozy cafes as you stroll through the winding streets.

Recommended accommodations:

No specific address, but look for charming guesthouses and boutique hotels tucked away in the streets of San Blas.

Tip: Be prepared for uphill climbs, but the spectacular views of the city and surrounding mountains are well worth it.

Sacred Valley

For those yearning for tranquility and stunning landscapes, the Sacred Valley beckons. This green area, which extends beyond Cusco, provides a pleasant respite while also serving as a strategic location for touring the Inca sites.

Advantages:

- **Scenic Beauty:** Wake up to stunning vistas of the Andes mountains and beautiful green valleys.

Recommended accommodations:

- **"Tambo del Inka, a Luxury Collection Resort & Spa":** This resort, located on Avenida Ferrocarril S/N in Valle Sagrado, Urubamba, offers luxury in the midst of nature.

Tip: While not in the city, the Sacred Valley offers a peaceful getaway. Consider it if you want to strike a balance between exploring and relaxing.

Cusco's Outskirts

Venturing a bit outside the city center opens up possibilities for more local experiences. Small neighborhoods on the fringes offer a glimpse into daily living away from the tourist crowds.

Advantages:

- **Authentic Local Living:** Engage with locals, discover hidden gems, and savor authentic cuisine away from the main tourist hubs.

Recommended accommodations:

Explore guesthouses and bed-and-breakfast options in neighborhoods like Santiago and Santa Ana.

Tip: Transportation may be required to reach the city center, but the immersive cultural experience is well worth it.

Recommended Hotels and Hostels

Now, let's go into specifics. Here are a few suggestions to get you started with your lodging search:

- **"El Mercado Tunqui"**

Address: Calle Siete Cuartones 306, Cusco

This beautiful boutique hotel, located near the lively Plaza de Armas, harmoniously blends the historical and contemporary. The rooms of El Mercado Tunqui reflect Cusco's rich heritage, combining traditional design with modern comforts. The hotel's rooftop terrace offers breathtaking views of the city, making it a great place to unwind after a day of exploring. El Mercado Tunqui's courteous personnel and attention to visitor pleasure offer an enjoyable and culturally immersive stay.

- **"Wild Rover Hostel"**

Address: Calle Cuesta Santa Ana 809, Cusco

Wild Rover Hostel is the place to go if you want to be in a dynamic and social environment. This hostel, located on a lovely street in the heart of Cusco, offers both dormitory-style and private rooms. The on-site bar supports a vibrant community by hosting frequent events and activities where guests may engage with other travelers. Wild Rover's personnel is noted for their warmth and helpfulness, making your stay not only relaxing, but also an adventure in and of itself.

- **"Belmond Hotel Monasterio"**

Address: Calle Palacio 140, Cusco

The Belmond Hotel Monasterio combines tradition and luxury. This five-star haven is located in the Plaza de Armas and was transformed from a 16th-century convent. The rooms combine colonial grandeur with contemporary elegance, providing a magnificent escape. The hotel offers superb dining options, a tranquil courtyard with a fountain, and a chapel with breathtaking murals. Immerse yourself in the luxury of the Belmond Hotel Monasterio for an unforgettable vacation in Cusco.

- **"Tambo del Inka, a Luxury Collection Resort & Spa"**

Address: Av. Ferrocarril S/N, Valle Sagrado, Urubamba

Tambo del Inka is a luxurious and serene refuge in the Sacred Valley. The resort, part of the Luxury Collection, has exquisite suites, a spa, and an outdoor pool with stunning views of the surrounding mountains. The Sacred Valley setting offers a serene escape while remaining close to Inca archaeological sites like as Pisac and Ollantaytambo. Tambo del Inka offers spa services, gourmet meals, and the opportunity to see the grandeur of the Sacred Valley.

Choosing the Right Accommodation for You.

Cusco has a broad choice of lodgings to suit different preferences and travel habits. To guarantee that your stay meets all of your expectations, let's look at some factors to consider while picking the ideal lodging.

- **Location, Location, Location.**

The first guideline of real estate also applies to travel! Consider where you want to spend the majority of your time. If you want to visit the historic center and Plaza de Armas frequently, staying in or near this region provides quick access to Cusco's heartbeat. For a more peaceful vacation, the Sacred Valley may be the best option.

- **Budgeting wisely.**

Your budget is an important consideration while selecting accommodations. Fortunately, Cusco caters to a wide range of prices, offering everything from low-cost hostels to opulent resorts. Determine your spending capacity and look at solutions that are consistent with your financial plan.

- **Amenities That Matter**

Different lodgings offer different amenities. Are you seeking for a pool to unwind after a day of exploring? Is an on-site restaurant appealing to you? Identify the amenities that are most important to you, such as free Wi-Fi, complimentary breakfast, or a spa.

- **Reviews and recommendations**

In the age of online reviews, it's wise to learn from the experiences of other travelers. Websites like as TripAdvisor, Booking.com, and Google Reviews can help you understand the advantages and disadvantages of each lodging. Expect frequent favorable reviews on cleanliness, service, and overall experience.

- **Local Flavor**

If you want to immerse yourself in the local culture, look for hotels that capture the essence of Cusco. Boutique hotels frequently combine historic beauty with modern amenities, offering a distinct and culturally rich experience.

Booking Tips and Tricks

Now that you've figured out what you're searching for, let's look at some tips and methods for arranging your lodging.

- **Book in advance, especially during peak seasons.**

Cusco, a major tourist attraction, has peak seasons. Consider booking your accommodations well in advance to ensure the best rates and availability. This is especially important if you intend to come around big celebrations or holidays.

- **Flexibility Can Save You Money**

If your travel dates are flexible, experiment with them during the booking process. Shifting your stay by a day or two can result in big savings, especially if you're willing to travel midweek.

- **Look for package deals.**

Many lodgings have package deals that include not just your stay, but also tours, food, and airport transportation. These can sometimes result in cost savings over booking each component separately.

- **Membership Discounts**

If you belong to a travel club, a loyalty program, or even a credit card program, look for special discounts or advantages. These can range from hotel upgrades to complementary amenities, which improve your whole experience.

- **Contact Directly for Special Requests**

If you have specific needs or questions, please do not hesitate to contact the accommodation directly. Whether it's a room preference or a dietary constraint, communicating ahead of time ensures that your needs are met, making your stay more enjoyable.

Choosing the right accommodation and employing savvy booking strategies will set the stage for a fantastic Cusco experience. So, examine your choices, plan ahead, and prepare to make memories in this enchanting city!

Choosing the appropriate lodging is like laying the groundwork for your Cusco journey. Each option has its own distinct charm, ensuring that your stay becomes part of the wonderful stories you'll tell with other tourists. So go ahead and choose the one that best suits your travel style, and let the enchantment of Cusco unfold before you!

Chapter 4

CUSCO'S TOP TOURIST ATTRACTIONS

Historic District and Plaza de Armas

Welcome to Cusco's core, where colonial architecture and cobblestone alleys bring history to life. The Historic District is a UNESCO World Heritage Site, with Plaza de Armas at its heart.

A Glimpse of Inca and Colonial Fusion

Plaza de Armas is a testimony to the intersection of Inca and Spanish traditions. The square is studded with centuries-old buildings, such as the magnificent Santo Domingo Cathedral and the Society of Jesus Church. Take a minute to appreciate the beautiful combination of indigenous and European aesthetics.

The Cathedral of Santo Domingo

Admire the Cathedral of Santo Domingo, a magnificent example of Spanish colonial architecture. The church, built on the foundations of the Inca palace of Viracocha, features beautiful woodwork and precious religious items. The chapels, each with its own tale, offer insight into Cusco's spiritual and artistic past.

Qorikancha: Where the Sun Meets Stone.

Qorikancha, located just a stone's throw from the Plaza de Armas, entices visitors with its mysterious appeal. The ancient Inca Temple of the Sun was previously decked with gold leaf, representing the Incas' devotion for Inti, the sun deity. Stand in astonishment as you see fragments of Inca masonry placed against Spanish architecture, a dramatic portrayal of the cultural tapestry woven into the Cusco environment.

Hidden Gems in Every Corner.

The Historic District is more than merely its major landmarks. Explore the narrow lanes packed with stores selling colorful textiles, homemade crafts, and local foods. Explore hidden courtyards filled with blossoming flowers, which provide peaceful respites despite the city's hustle and bustle.

Local artisans and street performers

The Plaza de Armas comes alive with the energy of local artists and street entertainers. Work with expert craftsmen to weave traditional textiles or carve beautiful pottery. Take a minute to appreciate the melodic songs of Andean instruments played by excellent players, which form a symphony that echoes throughout the square.

Cafes and Restaurants with a View

Enjoy a culinary adventure at one of the many cafes and restaurants surrounding Plaza de Armas. Choose a table with a balcony view for a delicious meal complemented by stunning views of the city and surrounding hills. The ambiance, combined with the great Peruvian cuisine, creates an unforgettable experience.

Cultural Events and Festivals

Keep an eye on the calendar, as Plaza de Armas holds a variety of cultural events and festivals all year. These festivals, which include vivid parades and traditional dances, provide a look into Cusco's vivacious character. Participate in the festivities, and you'll be immersed in the joyful rhythm of local life.

Nighttime Magic

As the sun sets behind the horizon, Plaza de Armas undergoes a magnificent change. Streetlights cast a warm glow over the area, creating a lovely atmosphere. Consider going on an evening stroll to see the colonial façade lighted against the night sky. Capture the romantic atmosphere and make enduring memories.

Sacsayhuaman

Inca Fortress: A Testament to Inca Ingenuity

Nestled high above Cusco, Sacsayhuaman is more than just a fortress; it's a testament to the Inca civilization's unmatched engineering prowess. Constructed during the reign of the ninth Inca, Pachacuti, in the 15th century, this fortress was a strategic military stronghold overlooking the capital city.

Megalithic Marvels: The Inca Stonework Mastery

As you walk through the site, the sheer scale of the stones used in Sacsayhuaman leaves an indelible impression. Some of these stones weigh up to 200 tons, yet they fit together with a precision that still baffles modern engineers. The Incas achieved this extraordinary fit without the use of mortar, showcasing an architectural precision that has stood the test of time.

Engage with local guides who share tales of the Incas' stone-cutting techniques and the symbolic significance of the three-tiered zigzag walls. The zigzag design is believed to represent the teeth of the sacred puma, an animal revered in Inca mythology.

Strategic Brilliance: The Military Significance

Sacsayhuaman's strategic location atop a hill provides a panoramic view of Cusco, enabling the Incas to spot potential invaders from a distance. The fortress served as a formidable defense, protecting Cusco from both internal and external threats.

Explore the zigzag walls, which not only served a defensive purpose but also showcased the Incas' tactical genius. The interlocking stones created a formidable barrier, rendering traditional siege methods ineffective against this architectural marvel.

Rituals and Ceremonies: Spiritual Significance

Beyond its military function, Sacsayhuaman was a site of immense spiritual importance for the Incas. The expansive esplanade within the fortress witnessed grand ceremonies and religious rituals, especially during the Inti Raymi, the Festival of the Sun.

Inti Raymi: Celebrating the Sun God

During Inti Raymi, the Inca people gathered at Sacsayhuaman to honor Inti, the Sun God, and seek blessings for a bountiful harvest. The esplanade transformed into a sacred space where priests performed ceremonies, and the Inca ruler himself participated in the rituals.

Today, you can almost feel the echoes of ancient ceremonies as you stand on the vast esplanade. Imagine the colorful processions, the rhythmic music, and the fervent prayers that once filled this sacred space during Inti Raymi.

The Mystery of the Towers: Lost and Rediscovered

One of the most intriguing aspects of Sacsayhuaman is the presence of three massive towers known as Muyuqmarka, Sallaqmarka, and Paucarmarka. These towers, aligned with the constellation of Orion, were believed to have astronomical significance.

Muyuqmarka: The Tower of Sacrifices

Muyuqmarka, also known as the Tower of Sacrifices, is particularly captivating. According to historical accounts, it was a place where ceremonial sacrifices took place. While the exact nature of these rituals remains shrouded in mystery, the site's energy evokes a sense of reverence and intrigue.

Panoramic Views: Capturing the Essence of Cusco

Climbing to the highest points of Sacsayhuaman rewards you with breathtaking panoramic views of Cusco and the surrounding mountains. The city unfolds below, revealing red-tiled rooftops, historic churches, and the meandering streets of the San Blas neighborhood.

Strategic Significance of the Viewpoint

The strategic placement of Sacsayhuaman allowed the Incas to survey not only the city but also the vast expanse beyond. This vantage point provided a crucial advantage for the Inca rulers, allowing them to govern with a watchful eye over their realm.

Photography Tips: Capturing the Magic

For photography enthusiasts, Sacsayhuaman offers a myriad of opportunities to capture the play of light and shadow on the ancient stones.

Visit during golden hour to witness the fortress bathed in warm hues, creating a surreal atmosphere that transports you back in time.

Preservation Efforts: Protecting the Legacy

Given its immense historical value, Sacsayhuaman has faced various preservation challenges over the centuries. Today, ongoing efforts by local authorities and international organizations aim to safeguard this cultural treasure for future generations.

Conservation Initiatives: Balancing Tourism and Preservation

As a responsible visitor, be mindful of the conservation initiatives in place. Stick to designated paths, avoid touching the stones, and respect any roped-off areas. Sustainable tourism practices play a crucial role in ensuring that Sacsayhuaman remains a source of inspiration for generations to come.

Sacsayhuaman: A Living Legacy

Sacsayhuaman transcends its status as a mere archaeological site. It's a living testament to the ingenuity, spirituality, and resilience of the Inca civilization. As you explore its ancient walls, participate in a guided tour, and absorb the mystical energy that permeates the air, you become part of a narrative that spans centuries.

Machu Picchu

Getting There

Scenic Train Ride

Taking the picturesque train ride from Cusco to Aguas Calientes is more than simply a mode of transportation; it's a visual feast. The route winds through the gorgeous Sacred Valley, providing stunning vistas of the Andean environment. Opt for the Vistadome train, which has panoramic windows and provides an intense connection to the spectacular surroundings.

Inca Trail Trek

Consider the classic Inca Trail hike if you want an adventurous and transforming experience. This multi-day walk is a pilgrimage in and of itself, passing through varied settings ranging from beautiful cloud forests to historic Inca stairs. Along the route, visit archaeological sites such as Winay Wayna to create excitement for the spectacular presentation of Machu Picchu.

Guided tours

Immersive narratives

Engaging a native guide at Machu Picchu is like unlocking the secrets of a living museum. These educated guides create storylines that bring the ancient city to life. Learn about the mysterious Intihuatana stone, which is thought to connect the city to celestial powers, and hear legends of Inca festivities that once rang through the terraces.

Timing Matters

To make the most of your Machu Picchu visit, plan your journey accordingly. Arriving early in the morning allows you to see the sun's first rays strike the old stones, producing a stunning interplay of light and shadows. Alternatively, an afternoon visit may provide a quieter setting and a more intimate relationship with the site.

Dos and Don'ts:

Respectful Exploration

Machu Picchu is regarded as sacred by both natives and visitors. To ensure respectful exploration:

- **Mindful Photography:** Capture the beauty without climbing on structures or touching ancient stones. The preservation of Machu Picchu is dependent on community responsibility.

- **Llamas & Wildlife:** While the llamas that graze the grounds are adorable, keep a safe distance. Respecting wildlife helps to ensure their survival as well as the preservation of the site.

Sustainable practices

Adopt sustainable practices during your visit:

- **Leave No Trace:** Stick to the principle of leaving no trace behind. To reduce your environmental impact, dispose of rubbish responsibly and follow specified channels.

- **Support Local Guides:** Look for local guides who are knowledgeable about the history and culture. Supporting local communities helps to ensure the region's long-term growth.

Beyond the Main Plaza

Huayna Picchu and Machu Picchu Mountain

For those who want adventure, consider climbing Huayna Picchu or Machu Picchu Mountain. These vantage spots provide spectacular views of Machu Picchu from various angles. Make sure to get your permits in advance, as the number of daily visitors is limited for conservation reasons.

Intimate Corners

Machu Picchu's appeal extends beyond the main plaza. Discover private areas such as the Temple of the Moon, a hidden jewel with beautiful stone sculptures. These quieter areas offer opportunities for introspection and a deeper connection with the site's spiritual aura.

Practical Tips

- **Weather Readiness**

The weather at Machu Picchu can be erratic, ranging from bright sunshine to misty rains. Pack layers, a waterproof jacket, and sturdy boots to ensure your comfort and preparedness for any weather fluctuations.

- **Tickets & Reservations**

Get your Machu Picchu admission tickets and any supplementary permits well in advance. To safeguard the site, there are limited daily quotas in place, underlining the significance of planning and scheduling ahead.

- **Altitude Awareness**

Machu Picchu is situated at an elevation of roughly 2,430 meters (7,970 feet). While lower than Cusco, it is critical to acclimate and stay hydrated. Take your time exploring and let your body adjust to the altitude.

Sunset and Sunrise Experiences.

Sunset at Sun Gate.

For a one-of-a-kind experience, arrive at the Sun Gate (Inti Punku) late in the afternoon. Watch the sun fall over Machu Picchu, putting a warm glow on the old stones. This less-crowded vantage point creates a quiet and enchanting ambiance.

Sunrise at Machu Picchu.

Alternatively, if you are an early riser, watch the sunrise above Machu Picchu. The first light of day bathes the city in a mysterious ambiance, producing a moment of awe and inspiration. Arrive early to guarantee your seat in the authorized dawn viewing zones.

Reflecting on Machu Picchu

Machu Picchu is more than just an archaeological site; it is a testament to human creativity and a portal to the spiritual worlds of the Inca culture. Take some peaceful time to absorb the spirit of this hallowed location, allowing its deep history to resonate with your own path.

Sacred Valley

Venture into the Sacred Valley, where time seems to stand still, and the legacy of the Inca civilization is etched into the landscape. This rich region, nestled between towering mountains, provides a tapestry of archaeological wonders, traditional marketplaces, and stunning landscape. Here's your guide to discovering the secrets of the Sacred Valley:

Pisac Market

- **Immersive Cultural Experience:** Pisac Market is not just a marketplace; it's a vibrant celebration of Andean culture. Arrive early to watch the locals set up their stalls, which are decorated with bright textiles, beautiful ceramics, and handcrafted jewelry.

Engage with the craftsmen, learn about their skill, and experience the rhythm of traditional Andean life.

- **Bargaining Tips:** Embrace the usual technique of negotiating in Pisac Market. Before entering into talks, take a stroll through the market to acquire a sense of price ranges. Approach sellers with a polite manner, and don't be afraid to negotiate; it's all part of the experience.

- **Must-Try Local Delicacies:** While exploring the market, indulge in local delicacies. Taste empanadas filled with flavorful ingredients and quench your thirst with chicha morada, a pleasant drink made from purple maize. Anticuchos, skewered and grilled meats, are a popular street dish.

Ollantaytambo

- **Living Inca Town:** Ollantaytambo is more than a historical site; it's a living Inca town where the past seamlessly integrates with the present. Navigate through small cobblestone lanes lined with well-preserved Inca walls and colonial houses. Watch villagers go about their daily lives against the backdrop of ancient ruins.

- **Ollantaytambo Fortress:** Ascend the terraced slopes to reach the formidable Ollantaytambo Fortress. This architectural masterpiece functioned as both a religious institution and a strategic military fortress. From the summit, take in the panoramic vistas of the surrounding valley, a tribute to the Incas' exquisite urban planning.

Tips for Exploration:

- Wear comfortable shoes because the terrain requires some uphill walking.

- Engage with local guides who can tell fascinating anecdotes about the town's history and culture.

Moray

- **Agricultural Innovation:** Moray, with its enigmatic circular terraces, is an agricultural marvel that showcases Inca ingenuity. The Incas employed these concentric terraces as an agricultural experiment, forming microclimates to test and cultivate diverse crops. The sight is both breathtaking and scientifically intriguing.

- **Photography Opportunities:** Capture the mesmerizing beauty of Moray, especially during the early morning or late afternoon when the sunlight casts shadows, accentuating the contours of the terraces. Moray's symmetry and form make it an ideal location for photographers.

- **How to Get There:** Accessing Moray may involve a combination of taxi rides and short walks. To ensure a pleasant and enlightening stay, consider hiring a local guide or joining a tour.

Museums and Galleries

Prepare to embark on a captivating journey through Cusco's cultural tapestry by immersing yourself in its diverse museums and galleries.

Museo de Arte Precolombino

Unraveling Ancient Masterpieces:

The Museo de Arte Precolombino, located in the magnificent colonial Casa Cabrera, is a refuge for fans of pre-Columbian art. Enter its halls, where ancient masterpieces from numerous civilizations, like the Moche, Nazca, and Chimu, are tastefully displayed. Admire the beautiful ceramics, textiles, and metalwork, each piece demonstrating the sophistication and artistry of these ancient cultures.

Interactive exhibits:

Unlike traditional museums, this institution promotes hands-on exploration. Interact with interactive exhibitions to gain a tactile understanding of the ancient procedures utilized to make these artifacts. Feel the touch of pre-Columbian fabrics, observe ceramic workmanship up close, and obtain a better understanding of the region's artistic creativity.

Temporal Exhibitions:

The museum periodically presents temporary exhibitions, so each visit provides a new viewpoint. From in-depth examinations of distinct cultures to themed demonstrations of ancient Peruvian technology, these shows revitalize the museum's already enormous collection.

Visitor Workshops:

Participating in one of the visitor workshops can provide a fully immersive experience. From pottery classes to textile weaving demonstrations, these programs offer hands-on experience with artistic traditions passed down through generations. Engaging in the artistic process not only broadens your comprehension, but also brings you closer to the Andes' rich cultural history.

Museo Inka

Journey Into the Inca Empire:

Nestled in the historic Casa del Almirante, the Museo Inka invites you to explore the intriguing world of the Inca Empire. The museum's collection spans centuries, providing a complete picture of Inca civilization from its humble origins to its pinnacle.

Archaeological treasures:

Discover the exquisite displays of ceramics, textiles, and metalwork that once decorated the life of the Inca nobility. Admire the golden treasures, which include jewelry and ceremonial pieces, each skillfully created to honor their own deities. The Museo Inka's collection offers a concrete glimpse into this ancient civilization's daily lives, religious practices, and social organization.

Quipus: The Inca Writing System.

The museum's collection of quipus, the unique Inca record-keeping system, is a standout feature. These beautifully knotted threads served as a means of communication and information storage. The Museo Inka provides a unique opportunity to see these quipus up close, allowing visitors to gain insight into the Inca Empire's sophisticated administration and accounting practices.

Mummy Room:

Enter the Mummy Room for an unforgettable encounter. Here, amazingly preserved mummies repose in ancient magnificence, offering light on Inca burial practices and their devotion for the afterlife. The strange yet interesting atmosphere adds another element of mystery to your understanding of Incan civilization.

Ethnographic section:

The museum's narrative extends beyond the Inca period to cover the great diversity of Peru's indigenous civilizations. The ethnographic part depicts the traditions and lives of modern Andean communities, developing an appreciation of the long-standing cultural history that continues to this day.

Chapter 5

EXPLORING CUSCO'S CUISINE

Hola! Welcome to Cusco, the hub of Peruvian culinary magic! As someone who has wandered through its cobblestone alleyways and experienced the flavors of the Andes, allow me to be your guide to the culinary delights that await you. In this chapter, we'll delve into Cusco's food, from traditional meals to hidden jewels, to ensure your taste buds have a wonderful journey.

Traditional Peruvian dishes

Lomo Saltado: A Dance of Flavors

Imagine soft beef strips waltzing with tomatoes, onions, and Peruvian spices, all perfectly stir-fried. Lomo Saltado is a culinary masterpiece that combines Chinese and Peruvian elements, reflecting the intriguing combination that characterizes Peruvian food.

As I sat in a quaint restaurant overlooking Plaza de Armas, the aroma of Lomo Saltado enticed me to savor each bite. Trust me, this dish is a must-try for any visitor.

Ceviche: Coastal Freshness in the Andes

Yes, you are in a city high in the Andes, but Cusco brings the seaside to you with its delicious ceviche. Fresh fish marinated in tangy lime juice and garnished with onions, cilantro, and a dash of spice—it's a blast of freshness that defies altitude.

I recommend visiting San Pedro Market for a real experience. Imagine yourself surrounded by locals as you enjoy this coastal treasure, an unexpected yet lovely surprise in the heart of the mountains.

Rocoto Relleno: Spice Up Your Cusco Adventure.

Rocoto Relleno is ideal for folks who enjoy spicy foods. This stuffed pepper, loaded with minced pork, veggies, and Andean spices, packs a hot punch that will have your taste buds tingling with delight.

I discovered this dish in a charming little restaurant near Sacsayhuaman, and it was a revelation. Accept the heat, and you'll find a symphony of flavors beneath the spiciness.

Best Restaurants and Cafes.

Cicciolina, a culinary oasis.

Cicciolina, located on Calle Triunfo and just a stone's throw from the bustling Plaza de Armas, is more than just a restaurant; it's a gastronomic haven. The warm, friendly atmosphere welcomes you in, laying the groundwork for a wonderful culinary adventure.

Menu: A Symphony of Flavors.

Cicciolina's food celebrates Peruvian delicacies while also drawing on other influences. Start your culinary journey with alpaca carpaccio or quinoa-stuffed mushrooms. For the main course, the melt-in-your-mouth alpaca steak or quinoa risotto demonstrate the chef's dedication to quality and inventiveness.

Ambiance: Elegance with a Touch of Bohemian

The restaurant is divided into several levels, each with its own unique atmosphere. The rooftop patio offers a panoramic view of Cusco's red-tiled rooftops and the distant Andes. The softly lighted room, filled with local artwork, creates a cozy atmosphere ideal for a romantic evening or a group of friends.

Insider tip: Make a reservation.

Given its popularity, booking a reservation is recommended, especially if you want a prime location on the terrace. The attentive service enhances the overall experience by providing menu insights and assuring a fantastic dining experience.

Address: Cicciolina, Calle Triunfo 393, Cusco, Peru.

Jack's Café - A Taste of Home

Jack's Café, located on Choquechaca Street just steps from Plaza de Armas, is a delightful establishment that flawlessly combines international comfort with Peruvian kindness. It's a sanctuary for people want to escape Andean flavors or simply crave a taste of home.

The Menu: International Comfort Food

Jack's Café offers a diverse cuisine to suit a variety of tastes. Whether you're craving a big breakfast, a warm sandwich, or a rich cup of coffee, you'll find it here. The menu includes familiar favorites such as eggs benedict, pancakes, and club sandwiches, providing a welcome reprieve for tired visitors.

Ambiance: cozy and inviting.

The café's warm environment, filled with diverse decor, exudes a welcome atmosphere. Wooden furniture and warm lighting make it a great place to rest after a day of exploring. The outside seating offers an excellent vantage point for people watching and soaking up Cusco's colorful vibe.

Insider tip: Go for breakfast.

Jack's Café is famous for its breakfast menu. Arrive early to enjoy their fluffy pancakes or the complete English meal. Pair it with a cup of their delicious coffee for an ideal start to the day.

Address: Jack's Café, Choquechaca 509, Cusco, Peru.

Chicha por Gastón Acurio: A Gastronomic Expedition

Chicha, located on the lovely Plaza Regocijo, is the idea of renowned Peruvian chef Gastón Acurio. This restaurant flawlessly blends classic Peruvian flavors with a modern touch, resulting in a culinary adventure that goes beyond the usual.

The Menu: A Tribute to Peruvian Diversity

Chicha's cuisine showcases Peru's gastronomic diversity, with dishes influenced by many areas and civilizations. Start your meal with the quinoa salad or corn cake appetizer. For the main course, the lamb stew or fish with Amazonian herbs will take you on a culinary tour through Peru.

Ambiance: vibrant and cultural.

Chicha's bright decor, complete with colorful murals and indigenous patterns, celebrates

Peru's rich cultural tapestry. The open kitchen lets you observe the culinary magic as professional chefs prepare each meal. The dynamic environment, along with live music on select evenings, makes Chicha a must-see for foodies.

Insider Tip: Sample the Pisco Sour

Pair your dinner with the classic Pisco Sour, a Peruvian cocktail made with the country's famous grape brandy. Chicha's bartenders are skilled at creating the ideal balance of sweet, sour, and foamy delight.

Address: Chicha por Gastón Acurio Plazoleta de las Nazarenas 210, Cusco, Peru

Green Point: Vegetarian Paradise.

Green Point, located on Carmen Alto Street, provides a unique perspective on vegetarian and vegan cuisine for those who are health-conscious and plant-based. Surrounded by vivid flora and a laid-back environment, it's a wonderful respite from meat-centric cuisine.

Menu: Wholesome and Creative

Green Point's menu is a creative showcase of plant-based ingredients. Indulge in their quinoa burger, rainbow salads, or Andean sushi rolls. The dishes are not only physically beautiful, but also flavorful, satisfying even the most discerning palette.

Ambiance: tranquil and eco-friendly.

When you walk into Green Point, you'll be met by a tranquil atmosphere filled with recycled and eco-friendly décor. The outdoor seating area, surrounded by lush vegetation, offers a peaceful getaway from Cusco's hectic streets. It's the perfect place for a relaxing lunch or dinner under the Andean sky.

Insider Tip: Try Andean desserts.

Don't miss Green Point's variety of Andean-inspired desserts. The quinoa pudding and lucuma ice cream are delectable endings to a nutritious, plant-based supper.

Address: Green Point Carmen Alto 119, Cusco, Peru

Street Food Delights

Anticuchos: Grilled Perfect on a Stick

As the sun sets and the streets come alive, follow your nose to the enticing aroma of Anticucho. These marinated and grilled beef skewers are a street food phenomenon that offers the most authentic experience possible.

I ran into a street vendor near San Blas who was perfectly cooking these delectable delicacies. Trust me, the combination of smoky tastes and delicate meat will leave you with an unforgettable street food experience.

Picarones: Sweet Endings in the Streets

Every gastronomic trip requires a sweet finish, which in Cusco takes the shape of Picarones. Imagine golden-brown fried dough rings with a generous dollop of syrup - dessert bliss.

I discovered these delicacies in the crowded San Pedro Market. The perfume alone is enticing, and the first bite takes you to a sugary paradise. Don't pass up the chance to satiate your sweet taste with Picarones.

Remember that every meal in Cusco has a tale to tell. From the historic origins of Lomo Saltado to the modern touch at Cicciolina, the city's cuisine is a tapestry of flavors waiting to be discovered. So, fellow adventurer, relish each dish, accept the unexpected, and make your culinary tour through Cusco a highlight of your travel story. ¡Buen provecho

Chapter 6

NIGHTLIFE AND ENTERTAINMENT

Welcome to the energetic and vibrant side of Cusco. As the sun sets over the historic city, Cusco becomes a kaleidoscope of lights, music, and activity. Let's dig into the center of the nightlife and entertainment scene, where incredible experiences and memories await us.

Bars & Pubs

Cusco's Pisco Sour Delight

Our adventure through Cusco's nightlife begins with a visit to the city's diverse taverns and pubs. Start your evening with Peru's iconic cocktail, the Pisco Sour. Head to Museo del Pisco, where experienced mixologists create this delectable concoction. The bar not only provides delicious beverages, but it also educates customers on the history and art of producing Pisco Sours. Cheers to a great night ahead!

Calle del Medio—Where the Night Unfolds

For a more informal and laid-back ambiance, head to Calle del Medio. This bustling boulevard is lined with pubs that cater to a wide range of preferences. Calle del Medio is a mixing pot of locals and tourists, with unique themed pubs as well as traditional watering spots. Join the audience, swap tales, and dance to the beats of Latin music at Mushroom Bar and Paddy's Irish Pub.

The View from Norton Rat's Tavern

Norton Rat's Tavern offers a combination of history and nightlife. Nestled in the San Blas area, this pub provides a friendly ambiance and a great view of Cusco from its patio. Enjoy a refreshing drink, chat with other tourists, and soak up the atmosphere of this one-of-a-kind location.

Live Music Venues

Folklore and Fusion at El Meson.

El Meson offers a soul-stirring experience with Peruvian music. This venue honors the Andean region's rich heritage through live folk music performances. El Meson shows Peru's musical tapestry, ranging from classic Andean melodies to contemporary fusions. It's more than just a performance; it's an audio voyage through the heart of the Andes.

Jazz Nights at Fallen Angel.

For jazz fans, Fallen Angel is a must-see. Tucked away in San Blas' artistic neighborhood, this unique venue is famed for its strange design and small jazz performances. Imagine drinking a martini surrounded by varied art and the soothing sounds of jazz filling the air. It's an experience that goes beyond time and place.

Latin Beats at La Esquina

La Esquina is the place to go if you want to dance all night to infectious Latin music. This lively nightclub is popular among both residents and foreigners. La Esquina's bright atmosphere, active dance floor, and many Latin music genres will leave you weary but joyful. Do not be startled if the friendly locals invite you to join their dance circle; it's all part of the experience!

Cultural Performances

Qosqo Center for Native Arts

Attending a performance at the Qosqo Center for Native Art will provide a broader understanding of Peruvian culture. This cultural hub presents traditional dance and music performances that tell the stories of Peru's indigenous communities. The bright costumes, rhythmic beats, and expert performers combine to create a captivating display that ties you to the country's rich cultural past.

Cusco's Contemporary Art Scene

Check watch current performances to learn more about Cusco's modern arts and culture. MATE - Museo Mario Testino periodically hosts events featuring a combination of classic and contemporary artistic expressions. Keep an eye on their schedule for performances that push the limits of creativity and provide a fresh perspective on Peruvian art.

Crafting Your Night Out

Nightlife Dos and Don'ts

There are a few guidelines for navigating Cusco's nightlife. Do embrace the local spirit by drinking different Pisco Sours and engaging in spirited conversations. Don't forget to respect local norms; while Cusco is vibrant, it's important to be careful of noise levels in residential neighborhoods.

Safety Tips for a Night Out

Cusco is typically safe, but like with any city, it is critical to remain careful. Stay in well-lit places, avoid excessive alcohol intake, and always keep an eye on your valuables. Most importantly, believe your instincts: if a place doesn't feel right, it probably isn't.

As the night falls in Cusco, you'll notice that the city's heartbeat is echoed by its dynamic nightlife. Whether you're drinking a Pisco Sour in a historic tavern, dancing under the stars, or taking in a cultural performance, Cusco's nocturnal offers are as diverse as its daytime marvels. So go ahead and let Cusco's rhythm lead you through a memorable night in this magnificent city. Cheers to new friendships, cultural revelations, and unforgettable moments!

Chapter 7

OUTDOOR ADVENTURES

Welcome to the heart of the Andes, Cusco, Peru. This is the chapter where we delve into the thrilling outdoor adventures that make this place a must-see for thrill-seekers and nature lovers both.

Hiking and Trekking

Inca Trail: A Journey Through Time

Picture this: You are standing on a trail utilized by the Incas centuries ago, surrounded by lush foliage and stunning views. The Inca Trail is more than a walk; it's a trip through time. The four-day walk takes you through a variety of environments, from cloud forests to high-altitude mountain passes, culminating in the breathtaking Machu Picchu. Tip: Spend a day or two acclimating in Cusco before going on this expedition to conquer the high altitudes.

Alternative Treks: Off the Beaten Path.

Cusco offers a unique trekking experience away from the tourists. Explore alternate hikes such as the Salkantay Trek, which offers breathtaking views of snow-capped peaks and passes through remote Andean communities. The Lares Trek is another hidden gem, winding through stunning scenery and offering a true peek into native Andean culture. These less-traveled roads allow you to engage with nature and history on a more personal level.

Adventure Sports:

Rafting: Conquer the Rapids

If you're looking for an adrenaline rush, rafting on the Urubamba River is a must. Navigate over exhilarating rapids surrounded by high Andean mountains and lush scenery. Whether you're a seasoned rafter or a beginner, the river has a variety of difficulty levels, making it an interesting trip for everyone.

Zip-lining: Soar Like a Condor

Have you ever imagined flying like a condor above the Sacred Valley? Zip lining in Cusco makes that dream a reality. Feel the wind in your hair as you fly over the verdant valleys, getting glimpses of old ruins underneath. It is not only an exciting experience, but it also provides a unique view on the region's natural beauties.

What to Do and Don't Do

Now that we've ignited your adventurous spirit, let's discuss the dos and don'ts of having a safe and fun outdoor adventure.

Dos:

- **Acclimate Gradually:** The high altitudes in Cusco can be challenging. Take it easy on your first day, stay hydrated, and consider munching on coca leaves, a native treatment for altitude sickness.

- **Guided Tours:** For the Inca Trail and other treks, consider hiring an experienced guide. They not only enrich your experience with historical context, but also protect your safety on the routes.

- **Respect Nature and Culture:** When trekking or participating in adventure sports, please respect the environment and local cultures. Leave no mark and immerse yourself in the vibrant culture of Andean communities.

Don'ts:

- **Underestimate Altitude:** Altitude sickness is no joke. Avoid strenuous activity on the first day, and listen to your body. If your symptoms are severe, descend to a lower altitude.

- **Solo Treks in Remote locations:** Although exciting, solo treks in remote locations carry risks. Stick to well-established paths or take guided tours if you're not familiar with the area.

- **Disrupt Wildlife:** Cusco's environments support a rich range of flora and animals. Avoid upsetting wildlife and keep a respectful distance.

There you have it, fellow adventurers: the ins and outs of outdoor activities in Cusco. Whether you're exploring ancient trails, battling river rapids, or flying through the skies, Cusco has something for every outdoor enthusiast. Remember to enjoy the thrill responsibly, while also respecting the natural beauty and cultural history that distinguishes Cusco from other adventure destinations. Prepare to create lifelong memories!

Chapter 8

WHAT TO DO AND NOT TO DO

I've had my fair share of adventures in Cusco, and I can tell you that this city is a treasure trove waiting to be discovered. So saddle in and prepare for some insider advice on what to do and, perhaps more significantly, what not to do in this magical location.

Respecting local customs.

Cusco, where traditions run through the cobblestone alleys like a living tapestry.

The inhabitants take pleasure in their rich cultural past, and following their practices is essential for making the most of your trip. When visiting churches and sacred locations such as the Cathedral of Santo Domingo or the

Qorikancha, remember to dress appropriately. A simple tip: bring a shawl or scarf to cover your shoulders. A modest gesture can go a long way.

In terms of gestures, a warm greeting can go a long way. Learn a few basic Spanish phrases—a simple "Hola" or "Gracias" can open doors and hearts. And, if you're offered a Pachamama ritual, in which locals honor Mother Earth, participate. It's an authentic experience you'll never forget.

Cultural sensitivity

In the heart of the Andes, cultural sensitivity is the cash that buys amazing experiences.

Cusco is a cultural melting pot, with influences ranging from old Incan traditions to Spanish. Accept variety and keep an open mind. While photographing the vivid scenes, ask for permission. Some locals feel that photographs may capture the soul, and recognizing this idea demonstrates cultural awareness.

When engaging in conversations, take a moment to understand the context. Avoid controversial issues such as politics or religion, unless your new friend initiates the conversation. And, my friend, leave preconceptions at home. Cusco is a city of surprises, and making assumptions may cause you to lose out on the actual essence.

Safety Tips

Exploring the cobblestone streets and hidden lanes demands a bit of street smarts.

Cusco is relatively safe, although as with any city, it is prudent to exercise caution. Petty theft can occur, so keep an eye on your stuff, especially in crowded areas such as markets. Invest in a solid backpack and stay mindful of your surroundings.

Cusco's high height further raises the risk of altitude sickness. Take it easy on your first day, stay hydrated, and enjoy coca tea, the native medicine. It works wonders, believe me.

When it comes to transportation, choose registered taxis or ridesharing services. Negotiate the fare before entering, and always have the exact payment ready. It prevents any misunderstandings and ensures a smoother voyage.

What To Do?

It's time to immerse yourself in the diverse experiences that Cusco has to offer.

- **Historic District and Plaza de Armas.**

This is where Cusco's throbbing heart is revealed.

Begin your adventure in the Historic District, a UNESCO World Heritage Site. Plaza de Armas, the main square, is a thriving metropolis surrounded by architectural marvels. Explore the Cathedral of Santo Domingo, a beautiful blend of Spanish and Inca design. Admire the beautiful features, and if you're lucky, attend a local event or festival in the square.

- **Sacsayhuaman.**

A castle in the heavens, where history speaks via ancient stones.

Sacsayhuaman is more than just a place; it is an experience. The enormous stone walls contain stories of Incan might and resistance. Climb to the top for a panoramic view of Cuzco. And, if your timing is correct, you can attend Inti Raymi, the Sun Festival, which takes place right here. It's a timeless spectacle.

- **Machu Picchu.**

The crown jewel and peak of Incan genius.

Machu Picchu is a must. Plan your trip carefully, whether with a guided tour or solo exploration. Watch the daybreak from the Sun Gate, and let the mist reveal the ancient city beneath.

Remember to respect the site by staying on specified trails and not climbing on the remains. This is a once-in-a-lifetime opportunity; make it count.

- **Sacred Valley**

The whispers of the past resound through magnificent landscapes.

Pisac Market is a treasure trove of handcrafted goods and local delicacies. Bargain with the vendors to bring home a piece of Cusco. Ollantaytambo, with its Incan castle, remains trapped in time. Moray, the agricultural terraces, is an example of Incan invention. Allow the Sacred Valley to work its magic around you.

- **Museums & Galleries**

Learn about Peruvian history and art.

The Museo de Arte Precolombino highlights the diversity of pre-Columbian cultures, whilst the Museo Inka delves into the Incan civilization.

Take your time, absorb the history, and admire the artistry that distinguishes Cusco.

What Not to Do

Avoiding these traps will result in a smooth and respectful exploration.

- **Disrespecting Sacred Sites**

Leave only footprints; take only memories.

Avoid touching or climbing on historic structures, particularly in areas like Sacsayhuaman and Machu Picchu. These locations are more than just sights; they are living reminders of a beautiful history. Maintain their integrity for future generations.

- **Ignoring altitude warnings.**

Conquer the heights, but do so intelligently.

Altitude sickness is a genuine problem. Do not underestimate it. Take it easy the first day, drink plenty of water, and indulge in coca tea.

Pushing too hard too quickly can make your adventure an unpleasant memory.

- **Disregarding Local Etiquette**

Respect the customs that are embedded into everyday life.

When in Cusco, follow the people' lead. If you are asked to a Pachamama ritual, accept it with thanks. Respect customs, whether it's taking off your shoes before entering a home or maintaining eating decorum. Integrate into the cultural mosaic for a more enriching experience.

There you have it, fellow adventurer. Cusco is more than just a destination; it's a journey through history and culture. By respecting local customs, remaining culturally sensitive, and following these recommendations, you're sure to make experiences that will last a lifetime. Now get out there and let Cusco work its magic on you! ¡Buen viaje!

Chapter 9

ITINERARIES FOR DIFFERENT TRAVELERS

Welcome to the heart of our travel guide - Chapter 9, where we dive into creating the perfect itineraries for various types of travelers. Whether you're a history buff, nature enthusiast, traveling with family, or seeking art and culture, Cusco has something special for everyone. Let's tailor your Cusco experience to match your interests and preferences.

Weekend Getaway: Immerse Yourself in Cusco's Charm

Embarking on a weekend getaway to Cusco promises a perfect blend of history, nature, and cultural richness. Let's break it down day by day for an unforgettable experience.

Day 1: Art and Culture Lovers

Morning:

Begin your day at the historic heart of Cusco, the Plaza de Armas. The morning sun casts a golden glow on the Cathedral of Santo Domingo. Marvel at the intricate architecture and immerse yourself in the vibrant energy of the square.

Afternoon:

Venture to the Qorikancha, the Temple of the Sun, showcasing the fusion of Inca and Spanish cultures. Explore the Museo de Arte Precolombino for a deep dive into the region's artistic heritage. Lunch at a local eatery, savoring authentic Peruvian flavors.

Evening:

As the sun sets, take a leisurely stroll through the San Blas neighborhood. This bohemian district is dotted with art galleries and quaint cafes. Wrap up your day with a cozy dinner, surrounded by the creative ambiance of San Blas.

Day 2: Nature Enthusiasts

Morning:

Rise early for a scenic drive to the Sacred Valley. Start at the Pisac Market, where local artisans showcase their crafts. Absorb the vibrant colors and purchase unique souvenirs.

Afternoon:

Head to Ollantaytambo, an ancient Inca town with well-preserved ruins. Enjoy lunch with a backdrop of towering terraces. Explore the archaeological site, feeling the echoes of Incan history.

Evening:

Conclude your day with a visit to Moray, marveling at the circular terraces. As the sun sets, the atmosphere becomes magical. Return to Cusco for a cozy dinner, reminiscing about the day's natural wonders.

Day 3: History Buffs

Morning:

Embark on a journey to Sacsayhuaman. The morning light enhances the mystique of this Inca fortress. Explore the massive stone walls and absorb the panoramic views of Cusco.

Afternoon:

Delve into the heart of Cusco's history at the Museo Inka. Uncover artifacts and exhibits that narrate the tales of the Inca civilization. Enjoy lunch in the nearby San Pedro Market, surrounded by local flavors.

Evening:

Wrap up your historical immersion with a guided tour of the historic district. Wander through narrow streets, learning about the colonial and Incan influences. Conclude your weekend with a delightful dinner in one of Cusco's charming restaurants.

Extras for Every Itinerary:

Cultural Tip:

Engage with locals, learn a few basic phrases in Quechua, and participate in any ongoing cultural events.

Photography Tip:

Capture the golden hours of sunrise and sunset for stunning photographs of Cusco's landscapes and architectural wonders.

Note:

These itineraries are flexible, allowing you to adjust based on personal preferences and unexpected discoveries. Cusco's magic lies in its ability to surprise and enchant at every turn.

Family-Friendly Fun: Creating Lasting Memories

Cusco isn't just for history enthusiasts; it's a playground for families seeking adventure and bonding experiences. Let's plan a family-friendly itinerary for an unforgettable trip.

Day 1: Exploring the Plaza de Armas

Morning:

Start your family's Cusco adventure at the Plaza de Armas. Allow the kids to run around while you appreciate the historic Cathedral of Santo Domingo.

Afternoon:

Visit the ChocoMuseo, where the whole family can indulge in chocolate-making workshops. A treat for the taste buds and a fun, educational experience for the little ones.

Evening:

Dine at a family-friendly restaurant around the Plaza de Armas. Enjoy traditional Peruvian dishes while soaking in the lively atmosphere.

Day 2: Pisac Market and Ollantaytambo

Morning:

Embark on a family road trip to the Sacred Valley. Explore the vibrant Pisac Market, where kids can interact with local artisans and pick up handmade crafts.

Afternoon:

Have a picnic lunch at Ollantaytambo, surrounded by ancient Inca ruins. Let the kids explore the terraces and imagine the stories embedded in the stones.

Evening:

Return to Cusco and spend a relaxed evening at a kid-friendly restaurant. Share stories of the day's adventures over a delightful family dinner.

Day 3: Cultural Exploration and San Blas Stroll

Morning:

Visit the Qorikancha and Museo de Arte Precolombino. Engage the family in interactive exhibits that bring the history and art of the region to life.

Afternoon:

Have a family-friendly lunch in the San Pedro Market. Let the kids choose their favorite snacks from the diverse stalls.

Evening:

Explore the artistic charm of San Blas. Visit the neighborhood's art studios and enjoy a family-friendly dinner in this bohemian district.

Extras for Family-Friendly Fun:

Family Bonding:

Engage in simple Quechua phrases together and learn about the rich culture of the Andean people.

Kid-Friendly Tours:

Look for specialized family tours or storytelling sessions that cater to the interests of younger travelers.

Local Parks:

Take a break in one of Cusco's parks, letting the kids play while you enjoy the surroundings.

Budget Travel: Experiencing Cusco Affordably

Discovering Cusco on a budget doesn't mean sacrificing the quality of your experience. Let's map out a budget-friendly itinerary without compromising on the magic of this historic city.

Day 1: Plaza de Armas and San Pedro Market

Morning:

Start your day at the Plaza de Armas, soaking in the architectural wonders without spending a dime. Capture the essence of Cusco with a stroll around this historic square.

Afternoon:

Head to the San Pedro Market for an affordable and authentic lunch experience. Explore the stalls, offering local delicacies at budget-friendly prices.

Evening:

Enjoy the evening at the Plaza de Armas, where local street performers often entertain without charge. Feel the vibrant energy of Cusco's main square.

Day 2: Free Cultural Sites and Local Eats

Morning:

Visit free cultural sites like the San Blas neighborhood. Explore the cobblestone streets, lined with art galleries and workshops, providing a cultural experience without a price tag.

Afternoon:

Choose a local eatery away from the tourist hotspots. Many smaller establishments offer traditional dishes at more affordable rates.

Evening:

Experience Cusco's nightlife without breaking the bank. Explore the bohemian atmosphere of San Blas in the evening, filled with music and local vibes.

Day 3: Scenic Views and Outdoor Exploration

Morning:

Take advantage of free panoramic views at Sacsayhuaman. Explore the site and absorb the breathtaking scenery without any entrance fees.

Afternoon:

Pack a budget-friendly picnic and head to the free-access areas of the Sacred Valley. Enjoy a meal surrounded by nature and ancient ruins.

Evening:

Savor a low-cost dinner at a local market or street food stall, embracing the authentic flavors of Cusco without straining your budget.

Extras for Budget Travel:

Free Walking Tours:

Look for free walking tours provided by local guides. It's an excellent way to explore the city and gain insights without spending money.

BYO Snacks:

Pack some snacks and water when exploring, saving money on impromptu purchases during your excursions.

Local Transportation:

Opt for public transportation or walking instead of pricey taxis. It's not only cost-effective but also a great way to experience the local lifestyle.

Art and Culture Lovers

Day 1:

Morning: Exploring the Historic District

Start your day with a leisurely stroll through the Historic District of Cusco. Marvel at the colonial architecture, vibrant markets, and the lively atmosphere of the Plaza de Armas. Immerse yourself in the rich culture by visiting the Cathedral of Santo Domingo, a masterpiece that blends Inca and Spanish architecture.

Afternoon: Qorikancha and Museo de Arte Precolombino

In the afternoon, head to Qorikancha, the Temple of the Sun. Witness the fascinating fusion of Inca and Spanish styles at this sacred site. Afterward, visit the Museo de Arte Precolombino to delve into the artistic achievements of the pre-Columbian cultures. Take your time to appreciate the intricate pottery, textiles, and sculptures on display.

Evening: Cultural Dinner and Folkloric Show

Wrap up your day with a cultural dinner at one of the local restaurants offering traditional Peruvian cuisine. Many establishments host folkloric shows, providing an immersive experience into the region's music and dance traditions.

Day 2:

Morning: Sacsayhuaman Exploration

Embark on a morning adventure to Sacsayhuaman, the colossal Inca fortress overlooking Cusco. As the sun rises, explore the impressive stone structures and marvel at the panoramic views of the city. Capture the essence of Inca engineering and soak in the historical significance of this archaeological marvel.

Afternoon: Artisan Markets and Street Art Tour

Spend your afternoon exploring the vibrant artisan markets of Cusco. Discover handmade crafts, textiles, and souvenirs that reflect the local artistry. Later, take a guided street art tour to witness the modern artistic expressions gracing the city's walls. Engage with local artists and learn about the contemporary cultural scene.

Evening: Tapas and Art Galleries

Wind down with an evening of tapas and explore the art galleries scattered around Cusco. Many galleries feature works by both local and international artists. Enjoy the fusion of flavors and artistic expressions as you unwind from a day filled with cultural exploration.

Day 3:

Morning: Machu Picchu Excursion

Embark on an early morning journey to Machu Picchu. While not in Cusco itself, this iconic Inca site is a must-visit for any art and culture lover. Let the guided tour unravel the mysteries of this ancient citadel, allowing you to appreciate the architectural marvels against the breathtaking backdrop of the Andes.

Afternoon: Artisan Workshops in Ollantaytambo

After returning from Machu Picchu, head to Ollantaytambo for an afternoon filled with artisan workshops. Engage in hands-on experiences such as pottery or weaving, connecting with the artistic traditions passed down through generations. Learn about the significance of each craft and create your own unique piece as a memento of your time in Cusco.

Evening: Dinner with a View

Conclude your art and culture journey with a dinner at a restaurant offering panoramic views of Cusco. Reflect on the artistic wonders you've encountered throughout your stay, surrounded by the illuminated cityscape.

Nature Enthusiasts

Day 1:

Morning: Sunrise at Machu Picchu

Begin your nature-filled adventure with an early morning trip to Machu Picchu. Witness the sunrise over the ancient citadel, bathing the stone structures in golden hues. Take a guided tour to understand the ecological significance of this UNESCO World Heritage site.

Afternoon: Exploring the Sacred Valley

After returning from Machu Picchu, venture into the Sacred Valley. Visit Pisac Market, where the colors of traditional textiles and local produce create a vibrant tapestry. Continue to Ollantaytambo, exploring the terraced ruins and connecting with the natural beauty surrounding this ancient Inca town.

Evening: Stargazing in the Sacred Valley

Wrap up your day with a stargazing experience in the Sacred Valley. Away from city lights, the clear Andean skies provide an ideal backdrop for observing constellations and learning about Inca astronomy from knowledgeable guides.

Day 2:

Morning: Hot Air Balloon Ride

Get an aerial perspective of the stunning landscapes with a hot air balloon ride over the Sacred Valley. Drift peacefully over archaeological sites, agricultural terraces, and picturesque villages. The morning light enhances the beauty of the valley, creating a magical experience.

Afternoon: Moray Agricultural Terraces

Explore the agricultural laboratory of Moray in the afternoon. The circular terraces, each creating a distinct microclimate, showcase the advanced farming techniques of the Incas. Wander through this unique site, surrounded by the natural beauty of the Andean highlands.

Evening: Traditional Peruvian Cuisine

Savor a traditional Peruvian dinner at a restaurant in the Sacred Valley. Many establishments focus on farm-to-table experiences, allowing you to enjoy the freshest local ingredients while surrounded by the natural splendor of the valley.

Day 3:

Morning: Bird Watching in Huacarpay Lake

For a nature-filled morning, head to Huacarpay Lake for a bird watching excursion. This serene environment is home to a variety of bird species, providing an opportunity for bird enthusiasts to spot Andean waterfowl and migratory birds.

Afternoon: Rafting on the Urubamba River

Experience the thrill of white-water rafting on the Urubamba River in the afternoon. This adventure combines adrenaline with the natural beauty of the Andean landscape. Professional guides ensure a safe and exciting journey for both beginners and experienced rafters.

Evening: Sunset Horseback Riding

Conclude your nature-focused itinerary with a sunset horseback riding experience. Ride through the scenic trails around Cusco as the sun sets behind the mountains, casting a warm glow over the landscape. It's a peaceful and picturesque way to wrap up your nature exploration.

History Buffs

Day 1:

Morning: Walking Tour of the Historic District

Embark on a morning walking tour through the Historic District of Cusco. Let the cobblestone streets guide you to architectural marvels like the Cathedral of Santo Domingo. Absorb the historical charm of the Plaza de Armas and delve into the stories behind the colonial buildings.

Afternoon: Qorikancha and Inca Museum

Visit Qorikancha, the Temple of the Sun, in the afternoon. Marvel at the precision of Inca stonework and the fusion of Inca and Spanish architecture. Continue your historical exploration at the Inca Museum, housing artifacts that provide insights into the daily lives of the Inca civilization.

Evening: Cultural Dinner in San Blas

Dine in the charming neighborhood of San Blas, known for its narrow streets and artisan workshops. Many restaurants in this area offer a blend of traditional Peruvian dishes and international flavors. Immerse yourself in the historical ambiance as you enjoy a cultural dinner.

Day 2:

Morning: Sacsayhuaman and Cusco's Archaeological Circuit

Start your day with a visit to Sacsayhuaman, the Inca fortress with colossal stone walls. Explore the intricacies of Inca engineering and take in the panoramic views of Cusco. Continue to Cusco's Archaeological Circuit, visiting sites like Q'enqo and Pukapukara, each with its own historical significance.

Afternoon: Traditional Textile Workshop

Engage in a traditional textile workshop in the afternoon. Learn about the ancient techniques used by the Inca to create intricate textiles. Create your own piece under the guidance of skilled artisans, gaining a hands-on appreciation for the artistry that has been passed down through generations.

Evening: Gastronomic Tour in Cusco

Embark on a gastronomic tour in the evening, exploring the flavors of traditional Peruvian cuisine. Visit local markets, street food stalls, and restaurants to sample a variety of dishes. This culinary journey offers a historical perspective on the fusion of indigenous ingredients with Spanish, African, and Asian influences.

Day 3:

Morning: Early Visit to Machu Picchu

Rise early for a transformative visit to Machu Picchu. Delve into the history of this ancient citadel with a guided tour, gaining insights into the rituals and architecture of the Inca civilization. Witness the mist lifting over the mountains, adding a mystical quality to your historical exploration.

Afternoon: Ollantaytambo and Chinchero

After returning from Machu Picchu, spend your afternoon exploring Ollantaytambo and Chinchero. Ollantaytambo, with its well-preserved ruins, provides a glimpse into the strategic planning of the Inca. In Chinchero, visit the colonial church and witness traditional weaving techniques, connecting the historical dots of the region.

Evening: Farewell Dinner with Andean Music

Conclude your historical journey with a farewell dinner accompanied by Andean music. Choose a restaurant that showcases traditional music and dance performances, creating a fitting finale to your exploration of Cusco's rich history. Reflect on the stories and ancient wonders you've encountered during your unforgettable stay.

Whether you're a history buff, nature enthusiast, family on an adventure, or a budget traveler, Cusco welcomes you with open arms, promising an unforgettable journey tailored to your unique interests. Enjoy every moment in this captivating city!

Chapter 10

SPECIAL EVENTS AND FESTIVALS

Inti Raymi (Festival of the Sun)

Cusco comes alive during Inti Raymi, an ancient Incan festival honoring the Sun God. Having witnessed this magnificent event, I can guarantee you that it is a cultural display unlike any other. Picture yourself immersed in a sea of brilliant colors, traditional clothing, and ancient customs.

The Essence of Inti Raymi:

Inti Raymi takes place annually on June 24th, coinciding with the winter solstice in the Southern Hemisphere. The festivities begin in Qorikancha, the Temple of the Sun, where performers dressed in extravagant Incan attire honor Inti, the Sun God. The enthusiasm is obvious as the procession progresses to Cusco's ancient Plaza de Armas, where rituals, dances, and ceremonies take place against the breathtaking architecture.

Tips for Inti Raymi:

- **Plan ahead:** Secure your tickets well in advance, as this event draws tourists from all over the world.
- **Dress the Part:** Embrace the spirit by wearing bright traditional attire found in local marketplaces.
- **Choose the Right Spot:** For the best views, arrive early in the Plaza de Armas or along the procession path.

Cusco's Annual Event Calendar

Beyond Inti Raymi, Cusco has a thriving calendar of events, each providing a distinct view into the city's personality.

- **Corpus Christi Procession:**

Imagine narrow cobblestone lanes covered with colorful flower petals and exquisite carpets produced by locals. During Corpus Christi in June, the city becomes a living tapestry as a huge procession of religious icons weaves through the streets.

- **Cusco Anniversary Celebration (Foundation Day):**

In late March, Cusco celebrates its foundation with parades, traditional music, and dance performances. The city's plazas transform into colorful gatherings, and people cordially welcome visitors to join in the fun.

- **Virgen de la Asuncion:**

Held in August, this event honors the Virgin of the Assumption. Pilgrims from surrounding regions go to Cusco for processions, traditional music, and a lively environment that reflects the city's profound religious traditions.

- **Christmas and New Year's Celebrations:**

Experience the holiday season in Cusco with a unique blend of traditional Andean customs and Christmas festivities. The Plaza de Armas is adorned with lights, and the inhabitants celebrate with music, dance, and, of course, great Peruvian cuisine.

- **Religious Feast of San Jeronimo:**

Held in September, this feast in the nearby town of San Jeronimo includes exciting processions, traditional dances, and a strong sense of community. It's an excellent opportunity to experience the cultural richness of the Cusco region.

Tips for Navigating Cusco Festivals:

- **Check the calendar:** Plan your trip around one of these festivals to fully immerse yourself in the local culture.
- **Respect Traditions:** Be respectful at rituals and processions, and seek advice from locals on appropriate behavior.

- **Capture the Moments:** Festivals provide fantastic photo opportunities, so keep your camera ready to capture the vivid colors and exciting energy.

Finally, Cusco's exceptional events and festivals add enchantment to an already intriguing place. Whether you're immersed in the grandeur of Inti Raymi or dancing in the streets during a local celebration, these events will definitely leave an everlasting impact on your Cusco adventure. Don't simply observe the city's varied cultural tapestry; immerse yourself in the rhythm of Cusco's festivals for a really remarkable travel experience. Share the fun, engage with the locals, and let Cusco's colorful atmosphere inspire your own travel tale.

Chapter 11

ADDITIONAL TIPS

We've wandered around Cusco's old alleyways, visited ancient sites, and eaten Peruvian food. As your travel companion, I've compiled some additional tips to ensure that your time in Cusco is not only memorable, but also seamless and hassle-free. So, let's get into the details that will help you on your trip.

Budgeting

Let's discuss money. Peru uses the Peruvian Nuevo Sol (PEN), and it's a good idea to have both cash and credit cards. Most locations take major credit cards, but having some local cash is useful, especially in marketplaces and smaller restaurants.

- **ATMs:** Cusco is dotted with ATMs, but it's essential to withdraw cash from reliable sources. To avoid unexpected surprises, stick to ATMs that are affiliated to banks. Inform your bank of your travel dates to avoid your card being flagged for suspicious behavior.

- **Cost of Living:** Cusco is generally affordable; however, prices might fluctuate. Expect higher pricing in popular tourist destinations. Make a budget for lodging, meals, transportation, and activities. Don't forget to allow room for any unexpected diamonds you come up along the route.

- **Haggling:** Embrace your inner negotiator, especially in marketplaces. While haggling is less usual in established establishments, it is part of the experience at sites like San Pedro Market. Be polite, smile, and enjoy the banter; it is both a cultural and a commercial transaction.

Photography Tips

Cusco is a visual feast, and you'll want to document every moment. Here are some pointers to ensure that your images capture the magic of this medieval city.

- **Altitude and Lighting:** Cusco's high altitude can have an impact on photography, but it also offers unusual lighting conditions. The sun can be quite bright, resulting in rich colors and dramatic contrasts. Experiment with different times of day to get the best shot.

- **Respectful Photography:** While the environment is beautiful, it is critical to respect the local customs and people. Always ask before photographing locals, particularly in indigenous cultures. Some may prefer not to be photographed, and it is critical to respect their desires.

- **Backup your memories**: With magnificent scenery and historical sites, your camera or phone will be working overtime. Remember to make regular backups of your images. Protect your memories, whether they are stored on the cloud or on an external hard drive.

Sustainable Travel Practices

As responsible tourists, we must protect the beauty of the locations we visit. Cusco, with its diverse cultural and natural legacy, demands our respect. Here's how you can support sustainable travel:

- **Responsible Trekking:** If you're going on a trek, consider operators who are committed to responsible and sustainable operations. Ensure they adhere to Leave No Trace standards, which protect the environment and local populations.

- **Eco-Friendly Accommodations:** Consider staying in eco-friendly lodgings that promote sustainable practices. Many hotels and lodges in and around Cusco strive to reduce their environmental impact.

- **Support Local Artisans**: When shopping for souvenirs, consider local artisans and markets. Avoid purchasing things derived from endangered plants or animals, and consider the environmental impact of your choices.

- **Water Conservation:** Cusco's water is a valuable resource. Conserve water whenever feasible, and bring a reusable water bottle to help limit plastic waste. Some hotels and restaurants have water replenishment facilities.

As our Cusco tour draws to a close, I hope these extra recommendations improve your travel experience. Budgeting intelligently, obtaining the right photo, and practicing sustainable travel are all factors that may make a big impact. Remember that Cusco is more than just a destination; it is an entire journey through history, culture, and natural beauty. Enjoy every moment, respect the people, and leave just footprints. Safe travels!

Chapter 12

BEYOND CUSCO

Day Trips and Excursions

Maras and Moray

Hola amigos! Now that you've experienced the colorful spirit of Cusco, let's venture beyond the city limits to visit the stunning Maras and Moray. Here's your guide to discovering these hidden jewels, as well as insider tips on how to get there.

Discovering Maras.

Maras, our first stop, is located about 40 kilometers northwest of Cusco. To get there, you can take a guided tour or book a private cab for a more personal experience. The gorgeous route leads you through the Andean scenery, providing glimpses of rural life and breathtaking views.

When you arrive in Maras, prepare to be charmed by the historic salt pans, known as the Maras Salt Mines. These tiered pools are a monument to Incan brilliance, having been skillfully built by hand over generations. Capture the contrast between the white salt and the natural surroundings, and don't forget your camera - this is an Instagrammer's dream!

Unraveling Moray's Mystery

Our next stop is Moray, which is near Maras. From Maras, you can take a local cab or join a guided tour that incorporates both sights. Moray's circular terraces, which resembled an ancient amphitheater, were used as an agricultural laboratory by the Incas. To explore the concentric rings, take a short hike and absorb the historical whispers of ingenuity beneath your feet.

Engage with locals in Maras and Moray to enrich your experience. Taste locally harvested salt or speak with a farmer—these interactions will make your journey genuinely unforgettable.

Rainbow Mountain

Prepare for a burst of hues as we travel to Rainbow Mountain, Vinicunca. Getting there takes an early morning departure from Cusco, and there are a few transportation choices.

Joining a guided tour is a convenient method to get to the trailhead, as it usually includes transportation, a guide, and any required permits. If you prefer independence, you can take a private cab or public transportation to the trailhead. The hike to Rainbow Mountain is strenuous yet enjoyable. As you ascend, the environment changes, revealing bizarre crimson, yellow, and lavender hues.

When you reach the summit, you will be met by the beautiful view of Rainbow Mountain. Layers of mineral deposits have formed a geological marvel. Breathe in the fresh mountain air, take some photos, and revel in your accomplishment of overcoming this natural wonder.

Pro Tip: Plan to acclimate in Cusco before embarking on the Rainbow Mountain trip. Stay hydrated and take it slowly—this isn't a race, but an experience.

Chinchero

Our final visit is Chinchero, a living testimony to Incan heritage and Andean traditions. Getting to Chinchero is simple, and you have a few options.

Consider taking a guided trip that includes Chinchero and other attractions, or hire a taxi for more flexible exploring. Chinchero is around 30 kilometers from Cusco, and the ride provides stunning views of the Andean scenery.

Cultural Immersion

Chinchero provides a distinct blend of history and local culture. Begin your journey with the Chinchero Market, which offers vivid textiles, handmade crafts, and traditional Peruvian items. Engage with the craftspeople, learn about their old weaving skills, and perhaps even purchase a keepsake or two.

Exploring Ancient Ruins.

Chinchero is also home to Incan remains that tell stories about a magnificent past. The archeological site includes agricultural terraces and a colonial-era chapel constructed on Incan foundations. Wander through the ancient stones, picturing what life was like in this high-altitude refuge.

Don't miss a display of traditional weaving at Chinchero. You will develop a deep respect for the expertise and creativity passed down through generations.

As our day tours and excursions come to an end, you'll have not only explored the heart of the Andes, but also learned how to traverse these treasures. Whether you select guided tours or self-directed exploration, these excursions beyond Cusco encourage you to touch with Peru's essence while experiencing the rhythm of life in the Andes. So, bring your sense of adventure and curiosity; there's always more to explore in this enchanted part of the earth. Until next time, adiós and safe travels!

CONCLUSION

My memories of Cusco are a kaleidoscope of ancient wonders, colorful markets, and welcoming locals. Cusco's ancient quarter, the Inca citadel of Sacsayhuaman, and the awe-inspiring Machu Picchu have all made for an unforgettable trip.

The city's culture, a tapestry of customs and festivals, enhanced my visit. Because of meticulous planning, navigating practicalities like as transportation and hotels was a breeze. Exploring the various cuisine, exciting nightlife, and outdoor excursions enhanced my trip.

Respecting local customs, following safety guidelines, and following itineraries customized to individual interests all improved the experience of my visit. Special events such as Inti Raymi and annual festivals boosted my cultural experience.

In saying goodbye, Cusco is engraved in my heart as a city that flawlessly merges history and modern vigor. To future travelers, enjoy every minute, relish the flavors, and let Cusco to make an indelible impression on your restless soul. Until our paths cross again, happy travels!

APPENDIX: USEFUL RESOURCES

Emergency Contacts

Medical Emergencies

In case of medical issues, contact the local emergency services and hospitals:

- Emergency Services: 911
- Hospital Regional del Cusco: [+51 84] 221292

Police Assistance

For any safety concerns or emergencies, reach out to the local police:

- National Police of Peru (Policía Nacional del Perú): 105
- Tourist Police (Policía de Turismo): [+51 84] 225876

Embassy and Consulate Information

For assistance related to your country of origin:

- U.S. Embassy in Peru: [+51 1] 6182000
- British Embassy in Peru: [+51 1] 6173000

Consulate Information

- Australian Consulate in Cusco: [+51 84] 231351
- Canadian Consulate in Cusco: [+51 84] 231735
- German Consulate in Cusco: [+51 84] 249813

Tourist Assistance

- Tourist Information Center (Centro de Información Turística): [+51 84] 223274
- Cusco Tourism Police (Policía de Turismo): [+51 84] 225876

Maps and Navigational Tools

City Maps

Navigate Cusco with detailed city maps available at local tourist information centers or your accommodation. Digital maps from apps like Google Maps and Maps.me are handy for real-time navigation.

Guidebooks

Carry a reliable guidebook like Lonely Planet or Rick Steves for in-depth information on Cusco's attractions, history, and local tips.

Offline Navigation Apps

Download offline maps and navigation apps to avoid data charges. Apps like Maps.me and Google Maps allow offline navigation after pre-downloading specific regions.

Tour Operators

- Cusco Expeditions: [+51 84] 608070
- Explorandes: [+51 84] 264132

Additional Reading and References

Historical and Cultural Background

Explore the rich history and culture of Cusco through additional reading:

- "Turn Right at Machu Picchu" by Mark Adams
- "Lost City of the Incas" by Hiram Bingham

Travel Blogs and Websites

Stay updated with firsthand experiences and travel tips from fellow explorers. Websites like TripAdvisor and travel blogs provide valuable insights.

Documentaries and Films

Deepen your understanding of Cusco with documentaries and films:

- "The Last Days of the Inca" (National Geographic)
- "The Motorcycle Diaries" (Film)

Libraries and Cultural Centers

- Biblioteca Municipal Cusco: [+51 84] 221025
- Centro Qosqo de Arte Nativo: [+51 84] 233986

Local Newspapers

- El Sol: Cusco's local newspaper

Useful Local Phrases

Greetings and Politeness

- Hello: Hola
- Good morning: Buenos días
- Thank you: Gracias
- Please: Por favor
- Excuse me: Perdón

Directions and Basic Communication

- Where is...?: ¿Dónde está...?
- How much does this cost?: ¿Cuánto cuesta esto?

- I need help: Necesito ayuda
- I don't understand: No entiendo
- Can you recommend a good restaurant?: ¿Puede recomendar un buen restaurante?

Emergency Phrases

- Help!: ¡Ayuda!
- I need a doctor: Necesito un médico
- Police: Policía
- I've lost my belongings: He perdido mis pertenencias

Shopping and Negotiation

- How much is this?: ¿Cuánto cuesta esto?
- Is there a discount?: ¿Hay algún descuento?
- Too expensive: Demasiado caro/a
- I'll take it: Lo/la tomaré

Ordering at a Restaurant

- Table for two, please: Una mesa para dos, por favor
- Menu, please: La carta, por favor

- I'm a vegetarian: Soy vegetariano/a
- The bill, please: La cuenta, por favor
- Delicious: Delicioso/a

Transportation

- Where is the bus station?: ¿Dónde está la estación de autobuses?
- How much is a taxi to...?: ¿Cuánto cuesta un taxi a...?
- I need a ticket to...: Necesito un boleto para...
- Is it far?: ¿Está lejos?

Cultural Courtesy

- May I take a photo?: ¿Puedo tomar una foto?
- Thank you for your hospitality: Gracias por su hospitalidad
- Can you recommend a local dish?: ¿Puede recomendar un plato local?
- What is the best time to visit...?: ¿Cuál es la mejor época para visitar...?

Health and Safety

- I need a pharmacy: Necesito una farmacia
- Where is the nearest hospital?: ¿Dónde está el hospital más cercano?
- I'm not feeling well: No me siento bien
- Allergic to...: Alergia a...

Socializing

- What's your name?: ¿Cómo te llamas?
- Nice to meet you: Mucho gusto
- Where are you from?: ¿De dónde eres?
- Cheers!: ¡Salud!

Language Schools

- Instituto Cultural Peruano Norteamericano (ICPNA): [+51 84] 249636
- Amauta Spanish School: [+51 84] 242523

Local SIM Card Providers

- Claro Cusco (Mobile Network): Located at various outlets in the city.
- Movistar Cusco (Mobile Network): Located at various outlets in the city.

Embassies and Consulates

- French Consulate in Cusco: [+51 84] 249987
- Spanish Consulate in Cusco: [+51 84] 224828

Ensure you familiarize yourself with these resources to enhance your safety, navigation, cultural understanding, and overall experience in Cusco. Happy and safe travels!

Printed in Great Britain
by Amazon